Let's Take Back Our Streets!

Let's Take Back Our Streets!

Chief Reuben Greenberg
Chief of Police, Charleston, S.C.

WITH ARTHUR GORDON

CB
CONTEMPORARY
BOOKS

CHICAGO · NEW YORK

A BERNARD GEIS ASSOCIATES BOOK

Library of Congress Cataloging-in-Publication Data

Greenberg, Reuben.
    Let's take back our streets! / Reuben Greenberg with Arthur
Gordon.
        p.   cm.
    ISBN 0-8092-4367-9 : $16.95
    1. Crime—United States.   2. Greenberg, Reuben.
3. Police chiefs—South Carolina—Charleston—Biography.
I. Gordon, Arthur.   II. Title.
HV6789.G84   1990
364.973—dc20   89-22052
                                                                CIP

Copyright © 1989 by Reuben Greenberg
All rights reserved
Published by Contemporary Books, Inc.
180 North Michigan Avenue, Chicago, Illinois 60601
A Bernard Geis Associates Book
Manufactured in the United States of America
International Standard Book Number: 0-8092-4367-9

Published simultaneously in Canada by Beaverbooks, Ltd.
195 Allstate Parkway, Valleywood Business Park
Markham, Ontario L3R 4T8 Canada

This book is dedicated
to the 350 members
of the Charleston police force
whose courage and zeal
have made it possible
to take back the streets
of our city

The only thing necessary for the triumph of evil is that good men do nothing.

—Edmund Burke

Contents

Let's Take Back Our Streets!

1
Let's Take Back Our Streets!

As a law-abiding citizen, how do you feel when you read in the newspaper (as you do all the time) that some convicted rapist or murderer, paroled because he is supposedly "rehabilitated," has raped or killed again?

How does it affect your blood pressure when you hear that another street hoodlum has been granted probation because it's his "first offense"—meaning only that it's the first time he's been caught?

How do you like it when plea bargaining waters down a sentence to a laughable tap on the wrist? Or when criminals who are a proven menace to society are set free to prey on us again because there's no room for them in jail?

How does it grab you when some bemused state legislature, urged on by starry-eyed liberals, decrees that unfortunate felons—poor things—are entitled to inhabit twice as many cubic feet of prison as before, thereby instantly reducing the capacity of the prisons in its jurisdiction by half?

What's your reaction when judges, yielding to God knows what influences or pressures, set aside their own original sentences to impose far milder ones? Or when defense lawyers delay the judicial process until the quest for justice collapses from sheer exhaustion, or perhaps because key witnesses have died?

I'll tell you how this makes *me* feel. Mad as hell!

As a police chief, I consider it an outrage when robbers, muggers, purse snatchers, and drug addicts roam the streets of our cities at night while ordinary citizens cower behind locks and bolts and burglar bars.

As a citizen, I find it insupportable when criminals coldly calculate—correctly—that the odds are in their favor that the law will not catch up with them, or will not punish them adequately if it does.

As an American, I am disgusted when I look at the latest FBI figures. Are you a home owner? Every ten seconds a burglary takes place somewhere in this favored land of ours. Do you drive an automobile? Last year stolen vehicles cost unfortunate car owners some six billion dollars. How many of these cases were solved? Fifteen percent. Which means the crooks' chances of being caught were one in seven. A tempting ratio. For the crooks.

Every thirty-eight seconds an aggravated assault (that's an assault designed to kill or maim you) takes place somewhere. The number of rape victims is up forty-two percent since 1977. There were an estimated twenty thousand murders in the past calendar year. These figures are not just alarming—they're sickening.

Yes, I'm mad as hell, but I refuse to concede that the war against the evil elements in our society is unwinnable. And I believe the worst mistake we can make is to assume it can't be won.

We can begin to reclaim those areas of our cities that have been abandoned to crime and to criminals.

We can begin to reverse the current of fear so that it is the criminal, not the decent citizen, who is afraid.

We can begin to take back our streets from the hoodlums, the muggers, and the drug dealers.

How do I know this? I know because I have seen it happen and I have helped to make it happen. Who am I to be saying such things? Let me introduce myself.

I am black.

I am a Jew.

And I am chief of police of Charleston, South Carolina.

2
Invitation to Wrath

Black. Jewish. Police chief in this proud old Southern city where the Civil War began. Later, I'll explain how a person of my background arrived where I am today. But first I want to offer you a formal invitation to join me in the sense of outrage and anger that I feel concerning crime in these United States. Unless you and a lot of other well-meaning citizens begin to be as mad as I am, mad as hell, we're not likely to make much of a dent in the situation nationally.

We've more than dented it here in Charleston. Some of the things we've done, some of our attitudes and our police techniques, need to be copied elsewhere. But that's not going to happen unless a significant number of private citizens open their windows—like the people in that movie *Network*, remember?—and scream out to the listening night: "I'm fed up! I'm furious! I'm not going to be pushed around like this! I'm not going to take it any more!"

If you don't think such anger is justified, take a good honest look at the way you—and most Americans—live.

Let's say it's three o'clock in the morning and you can't sleep. You've counted sheep. You've tried to read. You still have insomnia.

You stare out the window at the darkness that surrounds the house, and it occurs to you that a quiet walk around the block might relax tense muscles and calm taut nerves. But you know you're not going to do that. Whether you live behind locked doors in a run-down slum or behind a high-tech security system in a mansion on the hill, you're not going out to walk around at night. No way. Not you.

And why not? Because you're afraid, that's why.

You're afraid to walk your own streets because of the menaces—some real, some imagined—that lurk out there in the dark. Robbers. Muggers. Purse snatchers. Would-be burglars. Crack addicts ready to steal or maim or do anything for a fix.

You're afraid because gradually, imperceptibly, almost without realizing it you have accepted the premise that after dark the streets are not yours. They belong to the criminals.

Behind your locks and bolts and burglar bars you may have a fragile sense of security, but in reality you are living in a fortress, surrounded by other fortresses, none of which is impregnable.

Ask yourself in anger: is this really the land of the free and the home of the brave? Freedom still exists, all right, but in most places it's the criminal who has it. He is free to go out at three in the morning or any other time that suits him. He is not afraid of the law. He figures it will not catch up with him, or if it does the justice system will not punish him severely, if at all. He knows that you, the law-abiding citizen, have certain misconceptions that work steadily in his favor.

One misconception you have is that the criminal, since he is a human being, must be basically a lot like you. I can assure you that he isn't like you at all. You have been taught certain rules of decent behavior, and you abide by them. The criminal knows the rules, too—but he doesn't abide by them. You are accustomed to working for what you have. The criminal regards honest work with disdain. You know how to defer gratification when you have to. The criminal doesn't defer anything. He lives in a short time span. He takes what he wants when he wants it. Which is usually right now.

You may have the wistful notion that the criminal is the way he is because of poor environment, deprivation, social disadvantages. When you think this way, you rule out the critical factor of choice. There are many disadvantaged individuals who are not criminals because they *choose* not to be involved in crime. The criminal reverses this process; he calculates the risks, weighs them against the "rewards" of his criminality, then *chooses* to commit a crime because it seems to him the most cost-effective way of getting what he wants.

How should we react to such individuals? Not with resignation; that's what they count on. Not with the hope that they may overlook us and prey on somebody else; that's foolish, because no one is immune. Not with the naive view that redemption is always possible, even for the most savage of these predators.

No, our first reaction should be indignation, anger, righteous wrath. And our next reaction should be a determination to change things. Change things so that if these misfits break society's rules they must pay for it. If they won't impose accountability on themselves, we must do it for them. We must restore the concept of punishment to its rightful place as a deterrent to crime. We must face up to the fact that incarceration is the best answer we have been able to devise as far as habitual criminals are concerned. In our efforts to stamp out crime we need to be more intelligent, more innovative, more realistic. We don't have to be brutal, but we must not be afraid to be tough.

Otherwise the barbarians will take over even more territory than they already have.

3

The Good Guys Wear Blue

Some philosopher once said that a man is what he thinks about all day long. If there's one thing I think about all day long and most of the night, it's running a police force in a way that will enable it to catch the maximum number of crooks.

That's my job.

I like it.

And there are special occasions when I not only like my job, I love it, because there's a fierce satisfaction in being on the right side of human conduct and suppressing those who are not.

I remember, for example, a case that came up and knocked on my door at the very start of my career in Charleston. Actually, it knocked on the door of my automobile. I was driving my own car because my official car was in the shop for repairs. I had stopped for a red light at the corner of Meeting Street and Broad when a young black woman signaled that she wanted to talk to me. She was very agitated, very upset, shaking uncontrollably, her dark eyes full of tears. I couldn't imagine how she knew who I was, but she said right away, "You're the new chief of police, aren't you? I saw your picture in the paper."

You know as well as I do that there's something about a woman in tears that makes you want to help her. And there was something else, a flicker of hope in her eyes that stirred me deeply because I knew what that hope was: a black chief of police might be able or willing to help a black woman just a shade more quickly or effectively than a white chief might have been inclined to do. I knew that woman's eyes reflected the hope that my appointment had sent throughout the whole black community in Charleston. They were *counting* on me to change an old, unhappy climate of inequality, to begin to right some ancient wrongs. I don't think I consciously figured all this out as the woman poured out her story, but something deep inside me was aware of this hope and determined not to disappoint it.

The woman told me that she had come to the end of the line with her boyfriend. After years of enduring physical abuse from him, she decided to take their two children and go to New York, where she had relatives. She had even purchased bus tickets for herself and the children. But when she told the boyfriend she was leaving, he beat her—and to make sure she didn't leave, he took the baby away from her and brought the child to the home of his parents. He knew she would not leave town without the child. So the baby, in effect, was being held as a hostage.

The mother had gone to plead with the parents of the boyfriend, but they had refused to give the child back and had ordered her off the premises. In despair she had appealed to the Department of Youth Services, where bureaucrats sang their usual song: "There's nothing we can do." Then she had walked the streets, sobbing and shaking, until she happened to see me stop for the red light.

I put the young mother in the car and drove her to the police station. I would have liked nothing better than to go to the house, shove the guy and his relatives aside, and restore the baby to the mother. But I knew I couldn't. This was a civil matter, and under the law the father had just as much right to custody of the child as the mother. Still, looking at the tear-stained face and hopeful eyes of my passenger, I knew I wasn't going to join the chorus of the bureaucrats and say nothing could be done. I decided the key to handling the situation was somehow to transform a civil matter into a criminal one. Once it became a criminal affair, it would be in my jurisdiction and I could use the full force of the law against this bully.

First, I checked to see if he had a record. He did: aggravated assault, simple assault, shoplifting, drug possession. Next, I checked to see if there were any outstanding warrants against him. There were not. I asked the woman if he used drugs. She said that sometimes he used marijuana, but we couldn't just walk up and arrest him for that. No probable cause.

I asked the woman where we might be able to find this charming boyfriend of hers. She told me that he hung out at a joint on Cannon Street. He would be driving his brother's blue Chevrolet, she said. Then she added, "And he doesn't even have a license; it was suspended." This was the key: a suspended driver's license. I checked it. The woman was right. I called in one of our captains and told him what I wanted done.

The captain had doubts. We had never done anything like this before. Wasn't it a civil matter? Shouldn't the woman just go to Youth Services? By the look on his face, I knew he was silently asking himself, "Why is this new chief going to all this trouble? This is just another domestic dispute." His disapproval was obvious. Nevertheless, he sent two detectives to find the boyfriend.

The detectives found him holding up the wall outside his hangout on Cannon Street. The blue Chevy was parked a few feet away. The detectives waited in their car. After about half an hour, the guy walked over to the blue Chevy, climbed behind the wheel, waved good-bye to his buddies, and drove off.

In a flash, the detectives were on him. They pulled him over, arrested him for driving with a suspended license, brought him in, and towed away the car.

Now that the boyfriend was in custody and charged, we had a couple of hours to get the baby before the boyfriend got out on bond. With him in jail, and thereby incapacitated, the mother had sole custody rights, at least temporarily. That's what civil law says. I sent her, along with the two detectives, to the house where the child was being held.

The officers stood by as the woman told her boyfriend's parents that she had a right to take the baby because the father was in jail. The people refused. The detectives pushed them aside and let the woman get her baby. The family was in an uproar, yelling and screaming. Someone called the brother whose blue Chevy had been towed away. He walked up, learned what was happening, and belligerently demanded his car. He was informed that he could have it if he paid the towing charge. He told the detectives that the baby wasn't going anywhere until he got his car back. He reached for the baby. The detectives blocked him. He took a swing at the baby's mother and another at one of the detectives. They wrestled him down, cuffed him, and took him to the station. We thought it appropriate to put him in the same cell with his brother.

Four hours remained before the bus was to leave for New York. The woman and her two children had no place to go. Our Captain Ellington suggested letting them stay in the matron's quarters upstairs in the jail. The matron was glad to have the company.

When the time came, I instructed a detective to drive them down to the bus station, put them safely on the bus, and then follow the bus for at least an hour to make sure that none of the boyfriend's family tried to hassle the woman and her kids. Meanwhile, neither guy could make bond, so both stayed in jail.

I felt good about what happened, but some of the officers involved were dubious. Why go through all this trouble? They grumbled; it's not worth it.

That is where they were wrong.

It was worth it to that abused young mother.

It was worth it to a small black baby.

It was worth it to the city of Charleston.

And it was worth it to me.

The anger I've been talking about had found a legitimate target. It had brought about a change in the world in which we live. A small change, maybe, but a change for the better. Anger. That's what we need if we're to take back the streets and bend the curve of our civilization back upward.

It can be done. Let's begin to do it.

4
Burglars—America's New Leisure Class

One of the most common crimes we police are called upon to deal with is burglary; it happens at least eight thousand times a day throughout the land. It's also a crime that makes me very angry. It's heartbreaking and infuriating to go into the house of some poor woman who works hard all day and comes home to find the back door kicked in and her meager possessions stolen. Perhaps she has saved for months to buy a television set or has bought it on time. It was her only source of recreation or entertainment. Now it's gone, but she is still liable for the payments. The punk who stole it will sell it on the street for a fraction of its value. In a poor neighborhood, the owner is not likely to have insurance. In terms of callous indifference to the rights of others, to the suffering of others, burglars are in a class by themselves. And because the rewards are instant and the risks are low, it's a class that keeps growing.

Thanksgiving weekend, that most American of holidays, really is a time of rejoicing and gratitude—for burglars. Turkey Day always falls on a Thursday. By Sunday afternoon, the reports are flooding in:

"My garage has been broken into, and my outboard motor and all our bicycles are gone!"

"Our house has been vandalized and robbed; they took the microwave and my husband's shotguns and my jewelry, and they slashed some of my dresses and the sofa cushions in the living room, and they threw ink or something all over the walls!"

"We had all the doors locked, but they came in through a kitchen window, and they took the silver out of the dining room and our coin collection from the study and a .38 caliber pistol that we had in a bedside table."

The unhappy cries of rage and anguish go on and on. All the victims want us to catch the burglars and restore their belongings right away.

What few of the victims know, or would admit if they did know, is that they have probably contributed to their own unhappiness in one way or another.

First, they haven't stopped to think that over Thanksgiving schools are closed, which means that hundreds or perhaps thousands of teenagers are on the streets with nothing to do, and a percentage of these youngsters—not a large percentage but large enough—is going to be looking for an easy source of unearned cash.

They haven't given much thought, either, to the fact that professional burglars, who are by no means dumb, are aware that many families drive out of town to have turkey and dressing with Grandma or Great-Aunt Matilda, taking along not only the kids but the family dog, who may be toothless and decrepit but whose warning bark can give the most intrepid intruder pause.

They probably haven't bothered to have newspaper

deliveries stopped for the weekend or arranged for a neighbor to pick up the mail, so that a front porch littered with newspapers or an overflowing mailbox becomes practically an engraved invitation saying to the burglar, "See? Nobody's home. Come on in."

Some homes have burglar bars, and some have alarm systems of one kind or another. But most homes don't. Ordinary locks and bolts don't discourage the average burglar. One broken window pane and he's inside.

A generation ago, with the typical housewife at home all day with the kids, most burglaries took place at night. A married pair would be at home then, but they were usually asleep—not too much of a threat. Today, with both spouses working and the kids in school, the middle of the day is the logical time for a burglar to pay a visit. Neighboring houses are probably empty too. If a neighbor does see something suspicious, he's not very likely to call the cops. People have a strong disinclination to "get involved."

If you want a pretty good idea of how our criminal justice system works, or doesn't work, let me sketch for you briefly the ongoing career of Randy McQueen, black male, age twenty-three. Scene of operations: Charleston, South Carolina.

Randy first came to my attention in connection with a series of strong-arm robberies that took place in Charleston's Magnolia Cemetery, usually on Sunday mornings after church when LOLs (that's what we call little old ladies) were likely to go there to put flowers on a loved one's grave. Having been to church, they always had their pocketbooks with them. Randy's technique was simple and direct. Figuring correctly that no cops would be patrolling a cemetery on a quiet Sunday morning, he would hide behind a tombstone and wait until the LOL was bending over the loved one's

grave. Then he would jump out and slug her on the
back of the neck with his fist, hard enough to leave her
stunned, often with face bruised or eyes blackened from
violent contact with the headstone. He would snatch
the purse, flee through the cemetery discarding everything except the money, toss the purse into the bushes,
and be home before the victim's distress call could even
reach police headquarters.

Randy carried out several such assaults before we
staked out the cemetery and caught him. In February
1985, he was sentenced to serve five years and went to
prison.

Of course, no one expected him to stay in jail for
five years. South Carolina law says that a prisoner becomes eligible for parole after serving one-quarter of
his sentence. In view of Randy's propensity for slugging
LOLs, one might suppose that in his case parole would
be denied or at least delayed a bit. But one never knows.
Prison inmates are great con artists. Parole boards are
human. Jails are overcrowded, and there is no great
enthusiasm for spending taxpayers' money to build new
ones. So something has to give.

In this case the governor of South Carolina found
himself compelled by a federal court order to reduce
by 150 inmates the population of the prison where
Randy was languishing. By now it was August 1986.
Randy had served less than eighteen months of his
sentence. Nevertheless he managed to convince his jail-
ers that he was a sterling character, utterly rehabilitated
and reformed, who deserved to be among the happy
felons who would have to endure the hardships of over-
crowding no longer. Even as Moses once said to the
Pharaoh, so the federal court said to the governor, "Let
these people go!" So they went, and among them was
the ever-so-penitent Randy McQueen.

Presumably the felons released were the cream of the penitentiary crop—which makes one wonder about the caliber of those who stayed behind. In any case, when news of this mass exodus reached me, I sent a detective to check the identities of the prisoners who had been released. I wanted to know if any had been arrested or sentenced in Charleston, because I figured they would tend to drift back, or even hurry back, to their old haunts. The detective found that of the 150 released, ten had been arrested originally in the Charleston area. Of those ten we had records on six: photographs, descriptions, fingerprints, and so on. One of the six was Randy McQueen.

We didn't know at first, of course, whether McQueen had returned to our midst or not. We kept an eye out for cemetery assaults, but none occurred. There was a rash of burglaries, but there is always a rash of burglaries. I thought that if McQueen was going to return to his evil ways it would take him a few days or weeks to get started. I was wrong. He was released on August 21. On August 23 he carried out his first successful burglary. I'll say this for McQueen: he wasn't lazy. Of forty-eight burglaries committed in the following six weeks, he was responsible for thirty-five. Thirty-five burglaries in the same neighborhood! And we were lucky to catch up with him at that.

It happened this way. Detective Chisholm, the officer who had arrested McQueen in the cemetery, was amazed one day to see him walking down the street looking prosperous and unconcerned. "Hey, man, I thought you were supposed to be in jail!" "Not me; got out early for good behavior!" When this encounter was reported to me, a little light came on in my head. Had any fingerprints been found at the scene of any of the burglaries? Yes, in a few cases. We checked those prints against McQueen's prints. They matched. We picked him up. We explained about the prints. We told him he was a dead duck.

So dead, we assured him, that he might as well tell us about all the burglaries. So he did, guiding us cheerfully from house to house, including some places he had burglarized whose owners hadn't even reported thefts.

One thing puzzled me. "Tell me," I said to him, "you robbed one of these places twice. Why was that? Why'd you go back?"

He gave me a pitying look, as if conversing with a backward child. "To get the rest of the stuff," he said. He hadn't been able to carry it all away the first time.

Randy McQueen's methods were rather shrewd. Most daylight burglaries take place in the middle of the day. Partly because houses tend to be vacant then, with the owners at work. Partly because burglars don't like to get up early; they prefer to lie in bed congratulating themselves on their choice of such a deliciously high-profit, low-risk profession.

Evidently Randy McQueen had heard about the early bird and the worm. So he would walk down the street of some residential area and watch the cars of honest wage earners drive away. When no cars were left at a promising house, he assumed no one was at home. He would go around to the rear and kick the back door in—bam! He didn't worry about locks. He had strong legs.

He would go through the house, selecting TVs or VCRs or watches or microwaves or shotguns or whatever. He'd pile the loot just inside the front door. Then he'd calmly telephone for a taxi. When the taxi came, he might ask the driver to help him carry his belongings. If a police car came by and saw a taxi from a reputable company parked in front of a house with someone who seemed like the householder loading things into it, no suspicions were aroused. To improve efficiency, in at least one case, Randy McQueen took in the taxi driver as a partner. That way he didn't have to pay the taxi fare.

He had no trouble disposing of the loot. Most of it he sold on the street. A lot of people are willing to buy a hot TV set or a stolen pistol if the price is a fraction of its retail value. I have no doubt most of Randy's stolen merchandise was gone by nightfall. In fact, another burglar once told me that if he hadn't disposed of all stolen articles by sundown, he simply pushed anything left over down the nearest storm sewer. It was easier to get more stuff the next day than to keep the hot stuff overnight.

So Randy McQueen went off to jail again, but not too worried because he knew he would serve only a fraction of his sentence. And was he a sadder and wiser man? Well, wiser maybe. I remember asking him if he had anything to say before he and I parted company. Randy nodded thoughtfully. "Next time," he said, "I'll wear gloves."

5
Something *Can* Be Done About the Drug Problem

Contemptible though they are, burglars are only an ugly rash on the face of society. The real cancer is drugs.

Selling drugs illegally is a crime that makes most people very angry, and that includes me. The drug menace strikes at our homes, our schools, our children, even our law enforcement agencies. It threatens the whole fabric of society in a way that no other form of lawlessness does.

The anger people feel is reflected in the remedies proposed. Some call for a mandatory death penalty for drug dealers. Others say, Call in the Navy and sink their boats; call in the Air Force and shoot their planes out of the sky! One irate Congressman even advocated machine-gunning survivors from such sunken boats or downed aircraft. These furious reactions are neither practical nor even tolerable in a civilized society, but they're understandable.

It's customary to divide drug control into two main

categories: measures to curtail supply and measures to reduce demand. I'll talk a bit about these in a moment, but first I want to focus on a third area where we've had considerable success here in Charleston. This approach consists of interfering with or destroying the channels through which the drug traffic flows from the criminals who supply it to the customers who use it. Interdiction, we call it. Disruption of the lines of communication at the local level.

The best way to understand this approach is to think of the whole drug mess as a business—a sordid business destructive to many but highly profitable to others. In all businesses there must be a seller and a buyer. We have found it very hard to cut off the supply of drugs from the seller and, so far, equally hard to persuade the buyer not to buy. That leaves a third approach: separate the customers from the vendors. Create a barrier between them. Make it extremely difficult for them to deal with each other. If they can deal at all.

Visualize this: A drug dealer with a fistful of crack. A user with an outstretched hand full of money. And a blue-uniformed figure standing between them, making it very risky or very uncomfortable for the drugs to be exchanged for the money or vice versa. With this approach, no arrests are involved and no futile court proceedings are required because, as I'll explain, none are necessary. The link between pusher and user is actually a fragile one. At the local level, it doesn't take much to break it.

A little history on this whole drug situation will help make my point. The picture has changed tremendously in the past fifty years or so. Half a century ago, we had perhaps two hundred thousand drug addicts in this country. Dope fiends, we used to call them. They were a scruffy lot, easily recognizable. Then, as now, they killed and robbed each other frequently. They also committed various crimes to acquire money to feed their habits: shoplifting, burglary, robbery, passing bad checks, and so on. They were a problem, sure, but it was a problem that was mostly under control. Drug dealing was profitable, but no enormous sums were involved.

Today everything is different. In addition to the million to a million and a half addicts, we have a vast number of people—some say twenty-nine or thirty million—who are mainly recreational users of illegal drugs. They don't rob and steal to get the money; they have it already. Money earned from jobs of every kind: truck drivers and bankers, dentists and salesmen, stenographers and hairdressers. You can't spot them as users because they look just like the rest of us. They are not crime-committing users in the sense that they don't rob old men on park benches or break into homes, but I regard them with contempt and anger nonetheless, because these are the ones who make possible the enormous profits in the drug business. They are the ones who create the narco-millionaires and billionaires in Colombia or Mexico or Panama or Miami. Without them the drug problem would shrink back swiftly to containable proportions.

These are the people who speak disparagingly of crime in the ghettos and yet venture into sleazy places in the dead of night to make contact with their suppliers. And this is the pressure point that can be exploited: the point of exchange between vendor and customer. Here's how we do it in Charleston.

Most drug vendors are not anonymous; they are known to the police. The cops have arrested them before and have seen them post bond and return to their old neighborhoods almost instantly, to wait for trials that may not take place for months. The police have watched this dreary performance so often that they realize that arrest is not really the answer. The answer is to throw sand in the gears of the drug industry by making it difficult if not impossible for the customer to have access to the vendor.

One of our techniques is to put a tail on a known vendor. Not a plainclothes detective, but a uniformed cop. Wherever Johnny the Pusher goes during his "business" hours, the cop goes, too. He doesn't arrest Johnny, even though he knows the pusher is carrying narcotics. No probable cause. So when Johnny goes to Eddie's Bar and Grill, his favorite turf, the cop goes also. He does nothing, just stands there twenty feet from Johnny. Customers may come in, but they don't linger when they see a cop. They don't even say hi to Johnny. They go away and they probably won't come back. Not to deal with Johnny, anyway, because they know the cops are watching him.

Is there a known crack house in some low-income neighborhood? Same technique. No need for a full-scale raid. One uniformed cop strolling back and forth outside the house will put a noticeable chill on operations. Does this represent a strain on police resources? Not really. Using a single officer is far less expensive than using a squad of detectives armed with listening devices. Pretty soon that crack house is out of business.

That kind of surveillance puts extreme pressure on the vendors. What about the well-dressed banker who drives into the ghetto area at three in the morning to pick up a supply of cocaine for a weekend party he's planning? We have an answer for him, too. We call it a checkpoint, or a road block.

I'll tell you more about this extremely effective device later on, but for the moment let's say we have decided to conduct a traffic check between ten P.M. and three A.M. of all vehicles entering a certain district where we know an established drug pusher resides. We stop cars.

We ask drivers politely for licenses and registrations. We check equipment and usually find something wrong somewhere: a tail light out, a windshield wiper that doesn't work, a horn that doesn't blow, a registration that isn't signed on the back. So we give them a citation, and that establishes the time and place. Now we can prove that they were in this unsavory place in the dead of night, and they know that, and they fear the embarrassment that a newspaper account may cause.

Even if there's no cause for a citation, we ask the driver where he's going and why. If he gives an address, we can check the phone book and call the number on a cellular phone. If no one answers, then no one is at home, so why go there? If someone does answer, we usually say, "This is the Charleston Police Department. We have a person here, a Mr. So-and-So, who says he wants to visit you." When he hears the words "Police Department," the guy who answers will probably say he never heard of Mr. So-and-So. In that case, why should Mr. So-and-So go there? He may as well turn around and go home.

If Mr. So-and-So insists on exercising his constitutional rights to travel where he pleases, we say, "Okay, but just to make sure you're safe in this dangerous area, we'll go along with you and knock on the door."

In a minute, a uniformed cop is knocking on the door of the drug dealer's house. When that happens, you get all sorts of interesting reactions, such as the sound of toilets being furiously flushed. There goes the dealer's supply of drugs for the night. Sometimes he won't open the door at all. Is this a raid or what? Alarm and uncertainty have descended on that dealer.

Anyway, not many customers are going to be coming around from now on. The dealer may have to find another turf altogether. But most of the good turfs are already occupied by other drug dealers. This means our displaced dealer will have to fight the established dealer. Maybe, with luck, they'll shoot each other. More likely, one or both will begin to think that Charleston is a bad location and move somewhere else.

Meanwhile, back at the checkpoint, all sorts of fascinating evidence is coming to light. We can check with headquarters by radio to see if any warrants are outstanding against a driver. We can ascertain if he has had any previous arrests. We've arrested people for carrying and using drugs while on their way to get more narcotics. All sorts of suddenly discarded drugs have been swept up from the ground and confiscated. We've arrested people for drunk driving and for possession of stolen property. Right in the front seat of the car, we've found clothing and other items shoplifted from local malls with no receipts. And illegal guns, unregistered guns, concealed weapons. Some people have even left their cars and run away when they realized they were facing a search. Of course, we ran them down and caught them. All of which is just incidental to the main purpose, which is to interdict the flow of drugs.

You don't have to set up these checkpoints every night. Hit them one night, then leave them alone for two or three nights, then hit them again. You're creating uncertainty. You're dislocating a business operation. You're putting a very big question mark into the whole sales transaction. You're introducing the element of uniformed police, which is very important, because selling drugs is one of the few ventures outside of gambling and prostitution where neither the vendor nor the customer wants the police involved.

What about our national efforts to block the flow of drugs into this country? They're not very effective because, in a sense, it's an immigration problem and we have lost control of our borders. Cocaine isn't produced in this country. Heroin isn't produced in this country. These substances don't arrive here by intercontinental ballistic missile. They are brought in by people.

Every day tremendous numbers of people enter this country with virtually no control or real inspection. Experts on the subject say that no more than ten percent of illegal narcotics are seized. This may well be an optimistic figure.

Not long ago I was head of a committee of police chiefs who looked at the drug problem in a seminar in Phoenix. Representatives of the two hundred largest law enforcement agencies in the nation were present at that meeting. I asked the group a question: "If a total stranger came into your town, would it take him longer than two hours to be able to obtain cocaine? If so, please raise your hand." Not a hand went up. I asked another question: "Do efforts by the police in your community make it really difficult for people wanting drugs and able to pay for them to find them?" Again, not a hand was raised.

Additional proof of our failure to block off incoming supply is the fact that the price of drugs on the street is going down because supply is going up.

Don't misunderstand me, I think we should strike back at the drug dealers as hard as we can. Hit them where it hurts most: in their pocketbooks. Seize their assets whenever they can't prove that those assets were acquired legally. Seize their stocks, their bonds, their houses, their cars, their trucks, their racehorses. Seize their cash. Seize the motorboats that bring in the stuff from vessels lurking offshore. Seize the tractors that may be used to carve out hidden airstrips. Seize everything—and use the proceeds to intensify the war on this deadly form of crime.

Trouble is, so much money is involved that the narco-billionaires can easily accept such losses. Once, when I was stationed in Florida, I remember standing on a primitive landing strip far back in the Everglades and staring at a perfectly good airplane that drug smugglers had left there intact. The plane had landed its cargo all right, but it would never be able to fly out because the strip was too short. The drug dealers were aware of that when they flew in, but they didn't care. Perhaps the plane was worth half a million dollars. So what? If the cargo is worth a hundred million, who cares about the plane? They didn't even bother to torch it. They just left it there—and I found myself comparing their attitude toward the plane to the way a wino regards his bottle. As long as it has booze in it, it's the most precious thing in his life. Once it's empty, it's just a container to be tossed into the gutter. To the smugglers, that's all the airplane was: a container. Same for the expensive boats or cars or trucks that the smugglers use. Just containers for contraband narcotics. Disposable, if necessary.

It has been said that power corrupts, and absolute power corrupts absolutely. That's true of money, too; it has enormous power to corrupt when enormous quantities of it are involved. An officer working for me was once offered twenty-five thousand dollars—not to do anything specifically wrong but simply to call in sick and not show up for work on a certain night when the drug smugglers had scheduled an operation that they didn't want observed or interfered with. The officer reported this attempt at bribery, which took a lot of moral courage on his part, because we were paying him thirteen thousand dollars to work fifty weeks a year. He was saving up to buy a house for himself and his wife, and he figured it would take him five years to reach that goal. The smugglers were offering him a chance to get the money he needed in a single night— with virtually no risk at all. So where drugs are concerned, police officers often come under tremendous pressure. Not all of them can withstand it.

Here in Charleston we are close to the supply route that leads from Florida to the big cities of the north, but our local police are not involved in major drug busts as often as one might suppose; we leave that to the feds and other specialized agencies. I think our biggest score so far was the seizure of some twelve and a half pounds of cocaine worth about two million dollars, and that was mostly luck. Investigating what looked like a routine traffic accident, our patrolman found that the guy had a machine gun in the car with him. You don't need a machine gun unless you are carrying something that you fear may be stolen from you, something very valuable indeed. So a search of the car turned up the cocaine. I remember the driver very well. He was only about twenty-five, but the entire interior of his nose was burned away from snorting cocaine. The septum that separates the nostrils in most people was completely gone. Just one big ugly hole. Heavy drug use wreaks havoc on the human body. That's why you seldom arrest a real addict older than thirty-five. After the age of thirty-five, they're dead.

That's all on the supply side. On the demand side, I can visualize a much more imaginative and hard-hitting program of education about the really grisly results of using cocaine or heroin. Do you remember that article years ago in *Reader's Digest* called "And Sudden Death"? It was a description of a horrendous car crash so sickeningly vivid that it hit the reader with enormous impact. The effects of metal and glass fragments on human flesh were graphically portrayed. Some readers actually became ill reading it. But traffic deaths went down.

Suppose we took close-up color photographs of the nose of that junkie I was telling you about—the one whose septum was completely eaten away. Suppose we printed five million posters with those pictures and a big bold caption saying, "Do You Want Your Nose to Look Like This?" and pinned them up in every class-room in the country? Would that discourage some youngsters from getting started with drugs? You know it would.

I think our schools could tighten up on discipline all down the line. I know of one high school that gives a student a warning for the first infraction of the drug rules, suspension for the second, then expulsion for the third offense. But why wait for the second or third offense? That just gives the student one free shot at using drugs—or ten or twenty, so long as he isn't caught.

At times it seems to me that there's a not-too-faint undercurrent of hypocrisy running through this drug enforcement issue. We pass laws making the use or sale of pot illegal, but controls on our alcohol consumption are pretty lax. The effects of two or three martinis are similar to the high someone gets from smoking a couple of joints. A youngster may well ask himself, "What's the difference? You've got your favorite drug, Dad, and I've got mine. Only difference is, yours is legal and mine isn't."

We berate our Latin American neighbors for not doing more to cut off the flow of illegal narcotics. They reply that it is an insatiable American demand that causes the flow, not some sinister conspiracy by peasant producers of the coca leaf somewhere in Colombia. We ask our Mexican neighbors to spray paraquat, a power-ful defoliant, on their marijuana fields. They point out that it is against our laws to use paraquat on our own hidden marijuana plantings. So why should they?

We need to turn the climate around, the climate of acceptance where drug use is concerned, the attitude that what is happening is inevitable, the feeling that nothing can be done. That's the way a lot of people felt about racism thirty years ago. There were places in this country where it was not only tolerated, it was admired. Being a racist was understandable; it was okay; you could flaunt it; you could even be proud of it. But the efforts of thousands of people began to change all that. Racism became shameful, a sign of inferior breeding, inferior education. Oh, there's a lot of it left, probably always will be. But people don't go around patting themselves on the back for being prejudiced the way they used to. The climate has changed.

If we could persuade enough people that using crack or cocaine or heroin is basically stupid, that it's self-defeating, that only dummies get involved, that there's nothing glamorous about slowly killing yourself, then maybe the demand that fuels the whole sorry business would begin to drop. And eventually, the problem might become manageable. Demand is the key. Stop, or at least significantly diminish, the demand and you dry up the supply.

What about the well-meaning but misguided people who say we should throw in the towel and have the government distribute low cost narcotics to addicts, or even give drugs free to those who want them? I disagree completely with such proposals. The argument runs that free drugs would reduce crime, would put pushers out of business, would leave police free to deal with non-drug-related crimes. There may be some truth in such claims, but do we really want our government to supply ever-increasing quantities of drugs (most habits are progressive) to ever-increasing numbers of addicts? Do we want to be responsible for the innocent children born to such people—children who are themselves hooked on drugs? Can we be comfortable with the thought that the officials who supply those drugs will actually come to control those people's lives? Do we want to subsidize the demoralization of millions of our citizens rather than combat the drug epidemic with all the forces at our disposal?

I don't think so. I'm not ready to run up the white flag. We have proven in Charleston that we can make life very uncomfortable for user and vendor alike. We don't just rely on arrest and the snail-like performance of our courts. We use shame. We use embarrassment. We use fear. We use tactics that dislocate the drug business. We bring uncertainty and dread to the scum who profit by it and alarm and apprehension to those whose illegal purchases keep the whole miserable mechanism running.

It's a war. We may not be winning it at the moment, but we sure as hell can't afford to lose it. And some day, if we Americans put all our might and muscle, all our brains and determination into it, victory will be ours.

6
Off With Their Heads!

What crime in most communities is responsible for more than twice as many fatalities as homicide by knife or gun?

What causes far more numerous and serious injuries than fights or other forms of mayhem?

What results in more property damage and loss than all the activities of burglars and car thieves combined?

I'm talking about driving-under-the-influence traffic accidents and fatalities.

Driving under the influence of alcohol. Driving under the influence of drugs. If an epidemic of muggings, sexual assaults, or shootings broke out on the streets of most communities, outraged citizens would at once demand swift and effective official action. Nevertheless, that same threat to life and property arising out of the actions of drunk drivers seems to elicit only a small number of complaints. Unless, of course, the grim realities of driving under the influence of

32

drugs or alcohol are brought home by the serious injury or death of a loved one.

All too often the drunk driver is regarded with tolerance or indifference by otherwise thoughtful citizens whose unspoken reaction seems to be, There but for the grace of God go I. Indignation is muted. As a society, we appear reluctant to come down hard on drunk drivers. We despise and condemn serial murderers, but, aside from a momentary flicker of anger or disgust, we seem willing to put up with the person who in a single act may be responsible for more loss of life, more pain and sorrow, and more damage to property than any murderer with a gun in his hand.

Perhaps we soothe ourselves by referring to these homicidal episodes as "accidents." But there is nothing "accidental" about getting drunk and then driving an automobile. Both are deliberate acts. Drunkenness doesn't suddenly descend on someone out of the blue. No one is forced to take a drink at gunpoint. One becomes intoxicated by *deciding* to ingest alcoholic beverages or other drugs. Then one must *decide* to drive while under their influence.

That is what makes me so angry with these people. Getting drunk is stupid under almost any circumstances. Being drunk while operating an automobile on a public road is death-producing madness. The drunk driver who kills a victim has more than just an impact on the one whose life is lost. He or she also has an impact on the victim's family. Who will pay the mortgage? The note on the car? How will the children graduate from college? These tragic consequences become even worse when one considers that in almost all cases the whole incident could have been prevented.

People sometimes ask me why I get so incensed about drunk drivers. They wonder why I am so determined to arrest them—all of them—if I can. There's no way to bring all those people to trial, they say. Of course they're right; we can't bring them all to trial. But taking a drunk driver off the streets, even for a few hours, is a good thing regardless of whether he is ever brought to trial or convicted.

What's the answer? Harsher treatment. More severe penalties. In Sweden, the *first* arrest for drunk driving means loss of license. A measure was recently enacted by the South Carolina legislature that would authorize the seizure of an automobile owned by a thrice-convicted drunk driver when he is caught driving under the influence or with a suspended license.

Tough medicine? You bet. I was glad to see them pass that law. I hope they pass even harsher measures to be used when a driver continues to ignore the law and endanger the lives, hopes, and dreams of his fellow man.

Teach their children to regard them with scorn and contempt. Publish their names, regardless of wealth or social position, in headlines of shame. Lock them up and throw away the key. Off with the heads of the drunk drivers.

7

The Cops, The Public, And The Press

The whole thrust of our activities here in Charleston is to make the average law-abiding citizen regard the police as a friend and ally in the war against crime. We not only try to run down perpetrators, we also try to assist victims. We do a lot of things here that are not done anywhere else in the country.

For example, if we kick a door down on a warrant or in hot pursuit of a fugitive suspect, or if we damage furniture during a fight in somebody's living room, then we repair the door or the furniture. Most police departments don't do that. We do it because we find that the person who is arrested is almost never the owner of the property that's destroyed or damaged. It's his mother who owns the house, or someone else, so if we cause damage we're placing a burden on a third person. In most cases, this person is law-abiding. And yet as a result of police action, he or she might wind up having to pay several hundred dollars' worth of damages out of pocket. People tend to be alienated when they come out on the losing end in a police action.

If victims are burglarized or raped and afraid to sleep in their own home, we provide a hotel room and meals for several days until they feel more comfortable living in their house. It gives them some peace of mind while they decide what they want to do. If they need transportation to a relative's house, maybe fifty, one hundred miles away, and don't have any money, we'll put them in a patrol car and drive them to that relative's house. In other words, every time a citizen has contact with a police officer, it's not necessarily a negative experience. We're just as likely to be coming to repair a door as to break it down.

Or let's say a business is broken into at night. We try to get in touch with the owners, but if we're not able to find them we send a crew to board up broken windows or doors. That's what the owners would do if they were there. If we don't board it up, that gives other criminals the opportunity to come in. We can't put a policeman there all night to watch the place, or go by every half hour just to keep an eye on it. Neither procedure is practicable. We might as well do nothing. So we board the place up, and business owners seem to appreciate it.

We do whatever is necessary to meet reasonable needs. We don't ask citizens to pay us back; it's just a service we provide. Some police chiefs think this approach costs a lot of money, but it doesn't cost very much at all. Most people prefer to help themselves. And for those who can't, it's a very good thing. It probably costs us about four thousand dollars a year to do all the things I've mentioned, a small price for the tremendous police-community relations and good publicity we get.

We want people to see the police department as a

positive force in the community. We don't want them to watch a police officer nervously through the blinds of their houses. If it's their neighborhood, they're entitled to know what's happening. We don't tell people to "move on" or "break it up." We tell them, "Don't go home. Stay here and see what's happening." Nothing is going to happen that a citizen shouldn't see, and we may need that citizen as a witness. We gain nothing by sending good, taxpaying citizens away from the scene, leaving behind only cops and criminals as witnesses. We want to keep the neighbors there to observe what's going on, and let them see how we are protecting them.

There's nothing better than a civilian witness. I tell the cops here all the time, "If the only witnesses you've got are Sergeant Jones and Corporal Smith and Officer Mack, then you don't have any witnesses." I want a witness that a civil jury is going to believe, and that's somebody who is not involved. And the more witnesses, the more likely it is that the truth is going to come out.

Things have changed greatly in the black community here. A few years ago, black leaders were hesitant to condemn black criminals for fear of being considered traitors to their own race. Black-on-black crime was regarded as almost inevitable. Cooperating with police was practically unheard of. All that has changed.

In fact, I think the success we've had with law enforcement in Charleston over the last few years is based largely on our deracializing our war against criminals, particularly street criminals. The result has been the same level of response to everybody. Everywhere. I make sure that every officer in our department, black or white, understands that the percentage of people in a black neighborhood who are causing problems is very small. "Your purpose there," I tell them, "is to protect all the others. Your mission is to beat back the black criminal class and protect the black law-abiding citizens. And you can be successful because you're fighting only a very small segment of the community."

Just before I was appointed police chief, Charleston was the scene of heated racial tension stemming from some police shootings of black teenagers. But that's all behind us now. We haven't fired a shot in years. One guy was killed just after I came here, when he pointed a gun at police. But that shooting was such a clear case of self-defense, and there were so many civilian witnesses, that we were never accused of anything wrong.

Turning a police department around doesn't take years, or even months. It can be done immediately. I ended police brutality the first day I was on the job. Police officers are just like anyone else; they're very careful about whom they're nasty or abusive to, physically or verbally. If they think that you're somebody important or that you might cause them some trouble later on, they don't do it. It's necessary to let the officers see that *nobody* is so unimportant that they could assault him or her physically or verbally and get away with it.

We require officers to file a report when they even point their firearms at people, regardless of whether they fire them. If a gun is pointed at somebody, that's pretty serious because the next step after pointing a gun is firing it. Any officer who points a gun knows he will have to file a report explaining why. That's why our officers haven't fired a shot in over five years.

We discipline police officers for verbal abuse. Whether it's cursing people or calling them insulting names, there are no second chances. I discipline them the very first time they do it. I suspended an officer for that infraction after I was on the job for just three days. People were amazed. They said, "You mean just for cursing?" I said, "Yeah, just for cursing." If it had been the mayor or some important senator or congressperson or businessperson, they wouldn't have cursed. I had to show them that they couldn't get away with it. Consequently, in the last seven years, we've had only four allegations of verbal abuse. Only four times in a city that's forty-one percent black, and we've made thousands of arrests in that time. Those cops responsible were disciplined in all four cases. I'm just not going to give such people a second chance.

I hope it's obvious from what I just said how I feel about police brutality. I despise it. I hate it. I absolutely will not tolerate it among my officers. But I would like to say this too: I also hate it when police officers are unfairly accused of stepping over the line. I hate it when radicals or subversives or thugs of any description deliberately provoke a situation where the police have to be called in to control them and then scream in piercing tones trying to make the cops the villains and themselves the heroes. It's worse when all sorts of un-informed, woolly-minded liberals join in the chorus.

This happens more often than people suppose, especially in some of our larger cities. Often it is a calculated attempt to weaken public confidence in the police, and as such it is a step toward anarchy. Police *have* to use appropriate force when confronted with life-threatening violence—whether their own lives or the lives of innocent bystanders are at stake.

That threat is a constant hazard in police work. Not long ago the Mobil Corporation ran a paid announcement in The *New York Times* that contained some staggering statistics. In the past ten years, 1,525 police officers have been killed on duty, 204,584 have been injured, and 590,822 have been assaulted. In our war against crime, one American law-enforcement officer is killed in the line of duty every fifty-seven hours. Think of the wives, husbands, and children left behind. Then ask yourself if these brave people don't deserve all the gratitude and support you can possibly give them.

Well, to get back to Charleston.

I mentioned how black attitudes have changed here in recent years. White attitudes have changed too. People realize that crime is the problem of the whole community; you can't be indifferent to it no matter where it occurs. Ten years ago a common attitude among whites was, If black criminals attack other blacks, who cares? That's no longer the case. People do care. No man is an island.

Certainly the attitude of the crooks themselves has changed. They no longer think they can get away—literally—with murder. They know we have moved into neighborhoods where once they reigned supreme and taken those areas away from them. They know that if they snatch purses our Flying Squad will run them down no matter where they go. A lot of them have given up and moved to pastures that look greener. Good riddance.

The whole city is supportive of our efforts: the mayor, the city council, everyone. City officials are more crime conscious, more safety conscious. The director of our public parks knows, for example, that it's not enough to make a park neat and clean and appealing to the eye; it also has to be appealingly safe for citizens who want to use it. The city has moved into run-down slum areas and created office complexes with effective security control, where workers are not afraid to park their cars and walk to their jobs. And safety—like neglect and decay—is contagious. Set up an area or a complex that is safe, and adjoining neighborhoods begin to revive and imitate it.

The press deserves much of the credit. Soon after I took up my duties in Charleston, I remember, a grizzled old police chief of another municipality gave me some solemn advice. "Stay away from the press," he urged. "Keep a low profile. Have as little to do with reporters as you can. Things will go a lot easier for you if you do."

That's an attitude that still prevails on many police forces, but I think it's entirely wrong. The press is not the cop's enemy. It can make his job a lot easier, if a reasonable degree of mutual trust can be established. In my case, anyway, the advice was a little ridiculous. A black Jewish chief of police in Charleston, South Carolina? There was no way to pretend that wasn't news.

Reporters are always looking for color, and I don't mean skin color. They want news items that are colorful because they offer a break from the routine. In Charleston they were delighted when I issued track shoes to the members of our Flying Squad. They were intrigued when they found out I like to roller skate and sometimes tour the streets wearing my skates, but only on my own time. They were amazed when, answering a call to a traffic accident, I bumped the fender of a citizen's car and fined myself sixty dollars for reckless driving. Not an earthshaking event, perhaps, but that story was picked up all over the United States and even in parts of Latin America.

I'm convinced the worst thing a police chief can do, where reporters are concerned, is to try to stall them. If you have a sticky or controversial case, you have to give yourself enough time to assemble all the facts. Then call a press conference as soon as possible after the event and lay the facts on the line. The longer you wait, the easier it is for rumors to spread. Rumors of a cover-up. Rumors of police brutality. Once the rumor mill starts cranking out misinformation, it's almost impossible to stop it.

From a law enforcement point of view, the press can

have two very important functions. It can act as a monitor, a controlling influence. Of necessity, law enforcement operates harshly sometimes and law enforcement people sometimes abuse their power. A watchful press discourages this. In fact, by stripping people of anonymity, whether they are overzealous cops or leaders of a mob, the press almost automatically makes them more accountable and compels more moderate behavior.

The other function of the press is to give the public information that it needs concerning the whole crime picture. For example, are people really safest behind locked doors? Many think they are, and so the streets at night are deserted. Actually, the streets would be a lot safer at night if law-abiding citizens went out into them, not alone but in pairs or groups of three or four. The safest place in town is not necessarily where the police are patrolling constantly. The safest place is where people are, and the more people the safer it is. The press can help a great deal in disseminating information like that.

Balanced, accurate crime reporting is what every police chief in every town hopes for. We don't always get it. Reporters can imply that police work in a given case was less than satisfactory when they haven't taken the trouble to check out all the facts. I sometimes feel, too, that sensational stories about crime in the press or on television add unnecessarily to the fear the average citizen feels. Reporters have to report what happens, of course, but the way they report incidents can color readers' perceptions for years.

A lot of our success in Charleston, I think, is the result of careful planning, which includes anticipating the reactions of people and being prepared to deal with them.

I remember when some of us began to wonder why inmates of the jail couldn't do something more useful than sit and watch television all day. Why couldn't they be organized into working crews that could clean up run-down neighborhoods and make the city a more attractive place?

Soon, slum dwellers were amazed to see prisoners picking up trash around their homes. Gradually we expanded the operations to include other neighborhoods. Every taxpayer was glad to see prisoners doing something useful. I went out with the crews several times myself, fishing tin cans out of ditches. Once or twice our guards spotted and arrested criminals who had nothing to do with the clean-up crews but who nevertheless belonged in jail—an unexpected bonus. The point is, common sense and imagination and careful planning made the experiment work.

There are very few problems that can't be solved if you throw that combination at them.

8
How To Help The Cops
Help You

Whenever I tell a group of citizens that the police force needs help from them, someone always looks surprised, as if citizen-helping-cop is some strange reversal of a natural law. But the truth is, citizens can help the police in many ways.

Here's one so simple and so obvious that perhaps I should convey it in the form of a little drama entitled "What Took You So Long?"

Imagine this scenario occurring in your house late one night as you lie sleeping in bed. You are wakened by the stealthy rattle of the doorknob of your locked bedroom door. You reach hurriedly for the telephone. Thank God it's working! You dial the emergency number for the police. You tell them in a whisper that you live alone and that you are sure a burglar is in the house. You give them your address. You beg them to come quickly.

Still clutching the telephone, your heart beating fearfully, you wait as the seconds and then the minutes pass. You can still hear muffled sounds coming from other parts of your house. Now you hear the approach of an automobile. You begin to feel relief, but the car passes by. You peer out your bedroom window. In the glow of a street light you see that it is indeed a police car, but it has stopped some distance down the street. Again there is that sinister rattle at your bedroom door. You snatch up the phone again and tell the dispatcher that the police car has gone past your house.

Now you see the glow of a flashlight. Two officers are walking across the lawn of a house two doors down. Are they crazy? Why are they going to the wrong house?

Apparently the burglar sees the probing beam of the flashlight as well. There is the sound of running feet, a door opens and closes, someone is scrambling across the back fence. Now at last there is a knock on your front door. You look through the curtains and see a blue uniform. The other police officer with the flashlight is walking toward your backyard.

You open the door to let the first officer in. You blurt out, "The burglar got away—what took you so long— you went to the wrong house!"

The police officer says, "Sorry, sir. We didn't know which house was number 1234. None of the houses on this block have numbers on them."

It happens all the time. People want immediate assistance in an emergency from the police, the fire department, the emergency medical service. But they do little to prepare their homes so that they can receive that response. They fail to affix house numbers where they can be readily seen, their numerals contrasting sharply with their background surfaces, their size large enough to be seen clearly from the street.

Have you checked your own house number lately?

What about citizen arrests? If you see a young hood-lum snatch a purse, do you have the right to pursue him, apprehend him, hold him until the police arrive? Yes, you do have that right, but it is not always wise to act as self-appointed law enforcer. The miscreant may have a weapon and use it against you. He may even claim, later, that you used excessive force to subdue him and sue you for damages. Such suits occasionally are successful. In general, I would urge the concerned citizen to summon the police if possible or, if that is not possible, follow the suspect at a discreet distance, see where he goes, try to obtain his license plate number if he's driving a car, make mental notes as to what he looks like and how he's dressed, and turn this informa-tion over to the police as soon as possible.

Of course, citizen arrests occur all the time. Security guards, who now outnumber regular policemen in this country by a margin of about three to one, have no constitutional authority to make arrests. They may wear a uniform and carry a gun, but when they detain a shoplifter or a trespasser it is a citizen's arrest, not an official one.

What about booby traps? These devices are unlawful because they are more likely to injure a policeman or a fireman than a criminal. They are outlawed primarily because a mechanical device cannot distinguish the reasonable from the unreasonable entry. The "reason-ableness" standard requires that a *decision* be made to shoot a burglar and not that such shooting be automatic or the result of a mechanical response.

People sometimes say to me, "If I shoot a burglar and kill him outside in my backyard, do I have to drag the body back into my house to keep from being ar-rested myself?" The answer, quite simply, is no. A citi-

zen should not alter a death scene by removing or re-
positioning a corpse or any other evidence. It's unlawful
for anyone, including police officers, to move a body
except under instructions from the coroner.

Many people are under the impression that they are
allowed to defend themselves only if they are in the
confines of their home, but this is not true. People may
exercise the right of self-defense in any situation where
a threat to their own lives exists or a probability of
great bodily harm illegally directed against them can
be reasonably assumed. Traditionally such a threat has
to be "imminent," but in some recent cases it seems
that justice has been stretched to fit certain circumstances. In Detroit two men were charged with setting fire to a house in their neighborhood where drugs
were being sold. They were acquitted when their defense lawyers showed that following a shootout in the
street where children were playing, their pleas for protection were not answered by the police.

In my opinion, such drastic actions are not to be
condoned because they may well lead to vigilantism.
But they reflect the sense of rage and helplessness that
many citizens feel in response to the drug menace.

These extreme cases are the ones that make the headlines. What a chief of police really wants is a town where
the citizens are quietly vigilant. A crook can always hide
from the cops, but he can't hide from everybody. He
can't hide from the kid tossing newspapers onto front
porches in the hour just before dawn. He can't hide
from the jogger, the young mother pushing a baby
carriage, the nosy old lady behind the lace curtain in
her window. If the citizens of a town or city can be
educated to report a crime, identify the perpetrator,
and testify against him, that town is going to be a very
unhealthy place for crooks.

Educating citizens to get involved has to overcome

what seems to be a built-in tendency in most people *not* to get involved. A lot of that reluctance is fear of the unknown. If they take action to help the police, will they have to go to court? Will they have to testify? If they do testify, will the criminal or his relatives seek revenge? In all my career I have never known this to happen, but people are apprehensive anyway.

Sometimes people's inertia or indifference is truly astonishing. Not long ago, for example, two men invaded a neighborhood of Charleston in the middle of the night—it was about three in the morning actually— and proceeded to burgle a pharmacy. They broke down the door to get in. The owner, who had returned to the store earlier in the evening, had disconnected the burglar alarm and, unfortunately, forgotten to reactivate it. The robbers stole various things, including drugs. Then they turned their attention to a four-hundred pound safe.

The safe was locked, but it was conveniently equipped with rollers. If the pharmacy owner had removed one or more of the rollers, the safe would have been almost impossible to budge. But he hadn't. So the robbers rolled it out into the street, making considerable noise in the process. So much noise, in fact, that they awakened two young women who occupied an apartment above the pharmacy. The owner had rented it to them partly because he had hoped they would keep an eye on his property.

When they looked out the window, they saw two men trundling a safe down the street. But did they call the cops? Not at all. They peered more closely to make sure that their car, which was parked in front of the pharmacy, was not disturbed. When they saw that it was untouched, they went serenely back to bed.

Down the street went the robbers, the rollers of the

safe making such a racket that the thieves themselves became alarmed; they abandoned the safe in the middle of the street for a while and melted into the shadows. But when nothing happened, they came back and began pushing it again, this time toward their getaway car parked nearby with a third man at the wheel.

Opening the trunk of the car, the robbers struggled to lift the safe into it. They made so much noise that this time an accountant who lived on the street was awakened. He looked out and saw three men struggling with what he described later as "a big box." Strange men in a white section of town at three in the morning trying to lift some mysterious object, obviously very heavy, into the trunk of a car. Wouldn't that arouse suspicion in any even halfway intelligent person? Wouldn't it trigger a report to the police? Apparently not. The CPA watched them drive away. Then he went back to bed, slept the sleep of the untroubled, and didn't report anything to anyone until the following afternoon when he happened to go into the pharmacy and learned it had been burglarized.

That makes three eyewitnesses who chose not to get involved. Now at dawn here comes a delivery truck with a bundle of newspapers to be sold later at the pharmacy. The driver sees the front door of the pharmacy lying in the street. Not exactly the normal place for a front door. Obviously, a break-in has occurred. But does he report it? "No, man! Nothin' to do with me!" At least the driver had some reason, however farfetched, to fear he might become a suspect in the crime. The three other witnesses had no excuse—except perhaps apathy.

The safe was found eventually in the woods, where the thieves had cracked it open at their leisure. And an informant finally gave us a tip that led to their arrest. But how much easier it would have been if someone had simply dialed 911 and reported suspicious activity or an actual crime in progress.

Once in a while a criminal act may result in citizen involvement that brings out the best in the community. One February evening in 1984, a young woman named Nina Grego, a student at the College of Charleston, was driving her car in the downtown area. When she stopped for a red light, a holdup man approached her with a gun and ordered her to unlock the car door. When she refused, he fired at her point blank through the window. She had flung up her arm in a protective gesture. The small caliber bullet entered her armpit. Badly hurt, she managed to drive toward a nearby hospital, almost reached the entrance, then fainted from pain and loss of blood and collided with a street lamp. Police officers responding could see no visible wound; they thought the shattered window was the result of the collision with the lamppost. Only when she was brought into the hospital was the wound discovered. She was treated and eventually made a complete recovery. She gave a description of her assailant, but he was never apprehended.

James Grego, Miss Grego's father, a retired Navy officer, was understandably enraged by what had happened to his daughter. He decided to start an organization called Citizens Against Violent Crime (CAVE). When he placed an ad in the Charleston papers asking for support, the response was tremendous. Donations poured in from all over the state. Numerous other chapters were formed.

The original goals of CAVE were:

- increased prison facilities
- abolition of parole for violent crimes
- monitoring of courts to report on enforcement of existing laws

- reforms of the judicial system to increase concern for the victims of crime rather than the alleged rights of criminals
- development and enforcement of a Victims Bill of Rights

The members of CAVE stressed that they were not vigilantes; they wanted to work completely within the law. But, they said, "We are very angry, concerned citizens. We are mad and we are scared, but not so scared that we will surrender our cities. We will work within the system to change the system."

Within a few weeks, CAVE was receiving as many as a thousand letters a day. Since then it has had a real impact on the crime situation in South Carolina. It has brought about a dramatic change in the rate of parole in the state. When CAVE learns that a particularly vicious criminal is up for parole, it places ads in the paper urging people to oppose it. As a result, the percentage of applicants granted parole in South Carolina prisons has dropped from seventy percent to twenty-five and three tenths percent. CAVE is a striking example of how the tide can be turned against the criminal when concerned and angry law-abiding citizens get together and get involved.

CAVE has also come out in favor of popular election of judges. It carried out a six-month survey of circuit court judges to see which were the most lenient. The survey found that one judge handed down suspended sentences in seventy-two percent of his cases, while another made the same decision in only twenty-five percent of cases.

We have other citizen efforts in Charleston that increase the pressure on criminals. Crime Stoppers is an organization of businesspeople who pay rewards to informants for tips leading to the solution of a crime.

They too use newspaper ads as well as televised dramati-zations to good effect. Interestingly, only about a quar-ter of the informants ever claim the reward. Gradually the idea is taking hold that honest citizens can help not only the community but themselves by joining in the war against crime. After all, they are potential victims too.

In an effort to increase Charleston citizens' awareness of the role they can play in law enforcement, we have also run a series of half-minute television spots pre-pared by the National Institute of Justice. One, based on the famous (or infamous) Kitty Genovese case in New York, depicts indifferent witnesses who see or hear a young woman being murdered and make no move either to help the victim or alert the police. In another, sneering young hoodlums make it plain that the passive bystander, the uninvolved citizen, is actually their best friend.

These TV spots are usually aired late at night as public service announcements, so the number of viewers is not large. But effective crime prevention is the cumulative result of many small efforts. There is no single solution.

The magic number 911, now operative in at least eighty percent of the nation's largest cities, is an enor-mously effective weapon if citizens will just use it. When you dial 911, computers instantly identify the source of the call. If you are driving through an unfamiliar town and see a mugging or a purse snatching, you don't even have to know exactly where you are. Stop at the nearest public phone and dial 911. No coins are re-quired. Local cops will know the address; they can be there in minutes, sometimes even seconds.

Citizens often ask if their anonymity can be preserved when they dial 911. Yes, it can, although obviously it is better from a law enforcement standpoint if the caller is willing to testify later. Callers to such organizations as Crime Stoppers can also have their anonymity preserved, and usually do, although as I said before I believe that fears of reprisal in such cases are almost always unjustified. In all the thousands of cases I have observed firsthand since becoming a cop, I can't think of one where a criminal tried to retaliate against a witness. Once they get out of jail, which usually is all too soon, the crooks want to get on with their criminal careers. They're mainly interested in cash flow and the bottom line. They know there's not much profit in revenge.

Report. Identify. Testify. Make up your mind in advance to be willing to do these things. And don't be afraid to pick up the phone and dial 911. If you hear the sound of glass breaking in the dead of night, report it even if it's not in your own house. If you see suspicious-looking strangers in your neighbor's backyard, call in. If they turn out to be innocent in-laws from Peoria, so what? The cops won't mind; they'd rather check it out and make sure they're harmless.

I can tell you, from the point of view of a police chief, it's an exciting thing to see a trickle of information from ordinary civilians become a steady, useful flow. It's a heartening thing to see citizens who once regarded the police with fear and hostility begin to act as if cops are really their friends—which they are.

As these trends continue, the pressure on the crooks will increase. The National Institute of Justice has outlined the process: *Report. Identify. Testify.* And help us take back the streets.

9
Without Knowledge or Consent

I sometimes wonder if the average citizen ever stops to ponder the number of different functions the police department is called upon to perform. Not only routine things like chasing crooks or directing traffic or arresting drunk drivers. In just about every emergency imaginable, the first (and often the only) reaction is "Call the cops!"

Suppose an ill-tempered Bengal tiger escapes from the zoo and is seen prowling hungrily along Main Street . . . what to do?

No use calling the Humane Society; they'll say their cages aren't large enough.

Or the Game and Fish Commission; they'll say a tiger is not indigenous to North America and therefore not in their jurisdiction.

Or the Audubon Society; they'll say the tiger has no feathers.

Or the Fire Department; they'll point out that the tiger is not on fire.

Or the Army; they'll need instructions from Washington.

No, you do instinctively what all Americans are conditioned to do. You call the cops. And regardless of what the crisis is, out goes an officer in a blue uniform with a shiny badge and a trusty .38, while the one who sent him out (in Charleston, that's me) is left behind hoping to God that the officer is equal to the emergency, whatever it may be.

In an astonishing percentage of cases, we are. But where we cops are concerned, the area of responsibility keeps expanding all the time. The Bible tells us there is nothing new under the sun, but it seems to me that there is *always* something new under the sun. Consider, for example, the new and very deadly threat that our generation is facing. We call it acquired immune deficiency syndrome: AIDS.

Why should AIDS concern law enforcement officials? Isn't it a matter for health departments? Well, yes, it certainly is a matter for health departments, but when society tries to protect itself by creating laws designed to deal with AIDS, police are likely to be called in when such laws are broken. It's a brand new area of law enforcement, and one I became directly involved in only recently. Let me tell you how it came about.

Like every other city, Charleston has its gay community. Everyone knows by now that gay men are at high risk for AIDS. In many instances their lifestyles make them far more vulnerable than members of the so-called straight community. If a pair of homosexual men confine their sexual activities to each other and neither is infected by the AIDS virus, then they are in no danger. But promiscuous homosexual males certainly are.

My awareness of the problems posed by AIDS was

heightened not long ago when a local minister who specializes in counseling homosexuals came to me very worried about carriers of the AIDS virus who did not confine themselves to a single partner but had indiscriminate sex with many partners. In the minister's opinion, the threat was so serious that he wanted me to arrange to have notices posted in places frequented by gays emphasizing the dangers involved. I was obliged to tell him that his suggestion wasn't practical. The owners of gay bars or restaurants would not look kindly upon this form of publicity, and certainly the city fathers of Charleston would not be in favor of having such notices posted around town, either. But the pastor's visit did leave me more aware of the problem than I had been before.

The state legislature was aware of it, too. In May 1988 it became a felony in South Carolina for an individual with AIDS to knowingly expose another person to the disease through sexual intercourse without that person's knowledge and consent. I never dreamed that I would find myself operating under this statute, but almost at once I did.

It began when my secretary received a telephone call from a man who said he had to see me right away because he was giving serious thought to killing somebody. Naturally, this got my attention, and I had the man come in. Let's call him John Brown. Like most gays, he looked like any other individual. He told me that he was gay, that many people knew he was gay, and that he had had a gay partner—let's call him Harry Green—with whom he had lived until recently.

Unknown to John Brown, Harry Green had many other sex partners, and the time came when Green began to wonder if he had been exposed to AIDS. He went to the health department for a blood test, which revealed that his blood did contain antibodies to the

AIDS virus, very often indicative of the presence of the disease itself. Harry Green must have been shocked upon receiving such devastating news. Hoping that the test was wrong, he went back to the health department for another one. Again, word came back that his blood sample showed the presence of AIDS antibodies.

Harry Green did not tell John Brown about these communications from the health department. He did not want their relationship disturbed, so he hid the test results inside the cabinet of a stereo in the house they shared in North Charleston. And he went on with his sex life as before.

Now comes a most remarkable development. The stereo begins to function badly. One day, while Harry Green is out of the house, John Brown decides to take it out of its cabinet in order to have it fixed. Lo and behold, what does he find? He finds the two communications from the health department describing his lover's condition.

John Brown is understandably enraged. He confronts Harry Green and accuses him of being a carrier of the AIDS virus. Harry Green hotly denies it. John Brown produces the incriminating documents. Not only has his lover betrayed him, he may have infected him as well as others. A wild quarrel ensues. Finally, Harry Green admits that, knowing about his own condition, he continued to have sex with John Brown. John Brown maintains that Harry Green is a despicable person, devoid of conscience or moral scruples of any kind. Harry Green retorts that he is facing death and in the short time remaining to him intends to have as much fun as possible—fun in his case consisting mainly of homosexual relationships wherever he can find them.

This response provokes John Brown to white-hot fury. He decides to kill Harry Green. Not only will this be a just revenge, but a deadly menace will be removed from the gay community. John Brown knows that murder may have unpleasant consequences for himself, but he also knows that in South Carolina it takes at least eight years from sentencing to the imposition of the death penalty, and having now been exposed to the AIDS virus, he has good reason to suppose that he won't live that long anyway.

A very distraught and unhappy John Brown seeks out some of his friends in the gay community and tells them what has happened. Some of these, without the knowledge of John Brown, have also been sex partners of Harry Green. They agree fervently that he should be killed, as unpleasantly as possible, and there is a discussion of how this should be done. Perhaps if several different persons inflict stab wounds of varying severity (remember Agatha Christie's *Death on the Orient Express?*), it will be impossible to pin the blame on any single individual. Castration is suggested as a possible action. What about a beating so severe that he lingers for awhile and then dies in great pain?

All these solutions are appealing, but there are some cooler heads in the group. They have heard that there is a new law that might be invoked in a case like this. Why not at least go to the police and see what remedy might exist? Gays are not partial to police, as a rule; they don't like having their orientation revealed to the authorities. But John Brown and some of his friends are so incensed that they don't care.

They go first to the North Charleston police, since that was where the law was broken, most recently on the night before the discovery of the documents. But the North Charleston police are not interested. They don't know much about the new law or how it works. They tell John Brown that his problem sounds like a domestic quarrel. If a disease is involved, it's probably a matter for the health department. They don't think they have the authority to act.

John Brown then goes to the county police, since Green had also had sex with him numerous times in their jurisdiction. But the county police don't want to get involved, either. This leaves John Brown pretty well convinced that the law enforcement agencies are not going to act, and he might as well go ahead with his plan to kill Hary Green. Then someone suggests that, as a last resort, he talk to me. This leads to the telephone call and Brown's appearance in my office.

I'm aware that the new law was not broken in my jurisdiction, which ends at the Charleston city limits. But I agree with Mr. Brown that it is a very bad idea to have Mr. Green running around and possibly infecting a great many unsuspecting victims without their knowledge or consent. I also realize that the discovery of the reports from the health department was an extraordinarily lucky break, a million-to-one shot, on which it should be possible to build a very strong case against Mr. Green. If Mr. Brown will swear out a warrant, and if a magistrate can be found to sign it, Mr. Green's career as the Typhoid Mary of the gay community may come to an abrupt halt.

But here an interesting problem arises. Under South Carolina law, engaging in homosexual acts is in itself a felony. If Mr. Brown does sign such a warrant, alleging that Mr. Green broke the law by having sex with him without revealing his condition, would Mr. Brown not be incriminating himself? So—heavy irony—the new law designed to protect Mr. Brown might also put him in jail if he signs such a warrant. A catch-22 situation for Mr. Brown. But he is so angry that he says he doesn't care.

I call the health department. They say there is noth-

ing they can do. So I go to the prosecutor and explain
the situation. I tell him that we have a victim and a
complainant, but no warrant. I say that the offender
could probably be apprehended if there was a warrant
for his arrest, or an indictment, but I add that the
offense had taken place outside my jurisdiction. The
prosecutor says he will think about it and perhaps speak
to a magistrate about signing such a warrant.

Meanwhile, in our department we have a very able
female detective, Sergeant Nancy L. Fanning, who specializes in warrants. So I assign Sergeant Fanning to
the case. She is to make contact with members of the
gay community, win their confidence, ascertain the
whereabouts of Mr. Green and keep tabs on him, and
research the law and make sure it applies to the case.

This is no easy assignment. As a woman, Sergeant
Fanning is not likely to be welcomed with open arms
by the gay community. But she approaches the assignment with great tact and persistence. She learns that,
feeling the heat, Mr. Green has left town and allegedly
is living with his parents in another part of the state.
He is said to be thinking of leaving the country altogether and going to Australia, carrying with him his
ability to cause great harm through further sexual activities. Sergeant Fanning talks to Mr. Green's mother
and is assured that her son is not on the premises.
Sergeant Fanning is of the opinion that the mother is
lying.

The news that Mr. Green might flee the country im-
pels me to visit the prosecutor once more. We discuss
the case again; he is now willing to ask a magistrate to
sign a warrant. We decide that because of the jurisdiction question, it would be better for the county police
to handle the matter from this point on. I talk to the
chief of the county police, explaining that all the necessary preliminary work has been done; all he has to do

is send his officers with the warrant to arrest Mr. Green.

This is done. Now subdued and contrite, Mr. Green pleads guilty and expresses remorse for his actions. Nobody really wants him in jail, for obvious reasons, so he is given a sentence that amounts to house arrest; he is ordered not to leave home or to have sex; he is to ponder the total immorality of his former attitude and actions; his case is reported in the newspapers where perhaps the publicity will serve as a warning to AIDS carriers elsewhere.

Meanwhile, of course, Mr. Brown has had blood tests of his own. They are negative, but this does not mean that he is out of the woods. Symptoms of AIDS take time to manifest themselves. Sergeant Fanning is given a commendation for a job well done. I am left with the feeling that police detectives have done a job that, by rights, should have been handled by the health department. But when the cry goes up, "Call the cops," we try to respond and do what we can.

I am also left wondering how many individuals like Mr. Green may be sowing death indiscriminately and defiantly in hundreds—maybe thousands—of communities throughout the land.

Yes, there *is* something new under the sun. And I tell you, frankly, it scares the hell out of me.

10
Some of My Worst Friends
Are Lawyers

Just outside the door to my office in police headquarters hangs a little framed item:

> The other night a burglar broke into the Broad Street home of a prominent Charleston lawyer. And after a terrific struggle, the lawyer succeeded in robbing him.

Is this a true account of an actual happening? Well, no.

Is it intended to convey a certain disenchantment with lawyers on my part? Well, yes.

Indignation bordering on disgust where lawyers are concerned certainly didn't start with me; it goes far back into history. Shakespeare's Hamlet lamented "the law's delays." In *Utopia*, Sir Thomas More spoke of a community where "they allow no lawyers among them, for they consider them people whose profession it is to disguise matters." When the colony of Georgia was founded in 1733, its charter prohibited three things: rum, slaves, and lawyers. Not surprisingly, these noble guidelines didn't last long.

We have been conditioned, somehow, to speak with hushed respect for these interpreters of the law. But I think the public feels a lot of resentment toward lawyers that never really surfaces. People are convinced that lawyers charge too much, use language that is intentionally confusing, have little respect for justice and less for the truth. One bedeviled citizen is alleged to have said, "Lawyers are trained liars." So they are.

People might feel better about them if lawyers occasionally showed some indignation of their own, about murderers freed on some technicality or about rapists who, thanks to a "good" lawyer, go free to rape again. They never do. The public also grows weary of legislatures, made up almost entirely of lawyers, who are careful to block any legislation that might interfere with lawyers' opportunities to prolong litigation and collect fat fees. But what can the public do when the lawmaking process itself is controlled by the lawyers? Not much.

Perhaps I shouldn't let lawyers get under my skin to this extent, but they do. Some of them may be fine upstanding citizens, but others of them are not. Day in and day out, I encounter too many of the latter.

For example, not long ago a local attorney came to my office. He wanted to persuade me that aggravated assault charges against his client should be reduced to simple assault. The woman had attacked a police officer who was serving a warrant on her brother. The woman was black. Her attorney was white. The police officer in the case was also white.

When I refused to cooperate in having what I considered a life-threatening attack on one of my officers reduced to simple assault (which would have made a jail sentence very unlikely), the lawyer suggested that a racial issue might have been involved.

"What makes you say that?" I asked. "The mere fact that your client is black and the police officer is white doesn't make it a racial issue."

"Well," said the lawyer, "if you don't agree to a reduction in the charge, we're going to ask for a jury trial."

"Go ahead," I told him. "I think a jury will see that there's nothing racial about this case."

"Perhaps," said the lawyer. "But you may be sure that I'll raise the question of police brutality based on racial prejudice. And remember, you have to convince all twelve jurors that race wasn't a factor. I have to convince only one that it was. Just one, and you'll get a hung jury or an acquittal instead of a conviction."

That lawyer knew perfectly well that aggravated assault had taken place. But he was quite willing to introduce a spurious issue of racism in an attempt to get his client a reduced charge.

The case went to trial and we got a conviction, but I've never forgotten that taunt about the difficulty of persuading twelve jurors compared to the relative ease of persuading just one, because it seems like one more example of how the dice are loaded in favor of the defendant in criminal cases.

One reason they're loaded is that most legal talent gravitates toward the defense side—that's where the money is. And the publicity. And the accolades. Prosecutors are rarely heroes. In fact, your typical prosecutor is usually a young person fresh out of law school with little or no experience. He or she takes a job in the district attorney's office not to defend the public, but to gain experience and learn the angles so that he or she can wind up defending criminals. These attorneys move over to the defense side as soon as possible because, as a rule, being a prosecutor is not a promising career. Being a private defender is.

Losing a big case can damage a prosecutor's reputation. Defense lawyers can lose a dozen and not be hurt at all. But whether you're prosecutor or defender, the emphasis isn't really on justice. It's on procedures. That's what all the hairsplitting is about. A lawyer feels very uncomfortable if procedures aren't strictly followed. But justice? That's secondary.

I would like to see a system here more like the British one, where the guilt (or innocence) of the accused is more important than procedures. In England, for example, if the police obtain evidence by illegal means, the cops can be punished, but the evidence is admissible and can be used to obtain a conviction. That makes a lot of sense to me.

In my more charitable moments I remind myself that I read once that a lawyer is nothing but a businessperson. He or she provides a service, for a price. That service is to deliver what the customer wants. Like other businesspeople, lawyers don't ask their customers *why* they want what they want, or even if they ought to have it. Lawyers simply agree to try to obtain it.

In one way lawyers are better off than most businesspeople, however, because they collect their fees whether they are successful or not. Win their case or lose it, the price is the same. If a painter of automobiles botches a job, he is supposed to repaint the automobile without an additional charge to make good his promise of service. He must try again. But a lawyer who agrees to try again, by appealing a lost case, must be paid again, over and over, on and on, through the convoluted corridors of litigation. The rationale for this would be hard for the car painter to understand.

Sometimes I think lawyers can't even understand one another. Take a straightforward question, for example. Is a lawyer defending an accused felon allowed to remain silent while the defendant commits perjury, the lawyer knowing that it's perjury? Or does he or she have an obligation to see that the truth comes out? One would suppose that after two hundred years of American constitutional law and jurisprudence, a question as central and fundamental as this would have been answered long ago. But as recently as 1986 it was the question at issue before the Supreme Court in *Nix vs. Whiteside*.

The case developed in this way. Emanuel Charles Whiteside was facing a trial for murder in an Iowa court. In preparing for the case (he was planning to claim self-defense), he confided to his lawyer that, although he had not actually seen a gun in the victim's hand when he stabbed him, he nonetheless believed that the victim had one. The lawyer advised Mr. Whiteside that it was not necessary when establishing a claim of self-defense to prove that the victim had a gun in his hand. All he needed was a reasonable belief that the murder victim had a gun nearby, although no gun was actually present or found. The killer seemed to find this difficult to grasp.

Later, during preparation for the trial, the defendant told his lawyer that he had seen "something metallic" in the victim's hand. Asked about this new revelation, the defendant replied, "If I don't say I saw a gun, I'm dead." This, he said, was the way he intended to testify. His lawyer told Mr. Whiteside that if he testified falsely, it would be his duty as a lawyer to advise the court that he felt his client had committed an act of perjury. He said he would withdraw from the case unless his client told the truth. His client agreed to comply. So far, so good.

But when the defendant did tell the truth and was promptly convicted, he moved for a new trial, alleging that by advising him not to testify that he had seen a gun unless he actually thought he had seen one, his own lawyer had, in effect, joined the prosecution against him.

His motion for a new trial was denied. Upon appeal, the Iowa Supreme Court affirmed the conviction, holding that the lawyer's actions were not only permissible, but required under Iowa law. The defendant then took his case to the Federal District Court. There he was also denied relief, but he pressed on doggedly to the Federal Court of Appeals where—lo and behold—his conviction was reversed. This set of judges held that by threatening to reveal his client's confidences, the lawyer had violated the defendant's right to effective legal aid and thus his Sixth Amendment right to have "assistance of counsel for defense." They seemed to be saying that the lawyer had no obligation to ensure that perjury was not committed.

Finally, the U.S. Supreme Court heard an appeal of this decision. The highest court in the land reinstated the conviction, holding that the Sixth Amendment right to assistance of counsel is not violated when a lawyer refuses to cooperate with a defendant in his presentation of perjured testimony at trial. Said the Supreme Court, "The right to counsel includes no right to have a lawyer who will cooperate with planned perjury," a conclusion the average person in the street could probably have reached in two minutes or less. But think of the hours of litigation that were consumed as this particular case worked its way through the various layers of the judicial system!

Marvelous and devious are the ways of some lawyers who, having sworn to uphold the law, do their best to

evade it when their own interests are involved. I recall
one case in which a lawyer was the victim of a robbery.
He had met two young men in a public park and invited
them home for some unspecified entertainment. When
the men reached the lawyer's house and realized their
host was quite well off, they decided to forego the entertainment and rob him instead. They grabbed him,
tied him up, and proceeded to steal various antiques
and other valuable items.

Not long after the robbers left, the lawyer was able
to free himself. A quick survey of his home showed
that many valuable things were missing. But now he
faced a dilemma. If he reported the loss as a robbery,
he would be called upon to provide a description of
the criminals and perhaps explain under what circumstances he had invited them to his home. This he
did not care to do. On the other hand, if he simply let
the matter drop, he would be unable to recover anything through insurance. So he chose a third course of
action. He reported to us, the police, that he had returned to his home and found it burglarized. He said
he had no idea how the "burglars" had gained entry,
nor could he offer any clue as to their identity.

Not long after that, much to the suprise and no doubt
dismay of the lawyer, police detectives were able to
recover some of the stolen property. Subsequent investigation led to the arrest of the two criminals for another
crime. When questioned about the "burglary" at the
lawyer's home, the pair admitted to the crime, but in-
sisted it was a robbery, not a burglary.

How this information affected the lawyer's insurance
adjuster, I don't know, but there was a bizarre twist to
the whole thing. The father of one of the young hoodlums went looking for a lawyer to represent his son in
the second robbery case. The gods of irony decreed
that he should approach the lawyer who had himself

been the son's victim in the earlier crime. When the lawyer interviewed the boy, he realized right away that this was one of the young crooks who had robbed him. But a fee is a fee; the lawyer happily accepted the job and was forced to withdraw from the case only when a detective filed an ethics complaint against him. And, as far as I know, they all lived happily ever after.

I suppose at the bottom of my antipathy to lawyers lies the stubborn conviction that we should be allies in the war against crime, that they should constantly be doing things to make my job easier. But by and large, they do not seem to share my burning desire to put crooks where they belong—behind bars.

As I have said publicly more than once, if lawyers would put as much time and energy into convicting criminals as they do into defending them, the crime rate in this country would be cut in half.

But you can bet there'll be air conditioning in hell before that happy day arrives.

11
When Families Explode

The prevalence of domestic violence in American life had a lot to do with my choice of law enforcement as a profession. As a child, I witnessed numerous neighborhood fights between husbands and wives, or men and their girlfriends. The women almost always lost. They were the ones who suffered the black eyes, the busted lips, and the broken jaws. Often their only effective recourse was to flee to another city, or in extreme cases to resort to homicide to protect themselves.

The primary role of police forces in democratic societies is to protect those who are unable to defend themselves. This is why ultimately it must fall to the police to protect family members from spouse abuse, child abuse, and elder abuse. When violence explodes inside a family, there is usually only one swift solution: call the cops. Domestic abusers are cowardly as well as vicious. They choose their victims carefully. They attack the weak, the ill, and the defenseless. We police are often the first and only outsiders to become involved with these people. We understand, as few others can, the magnitude of the problem and how it pervades every class, race, and occupational group in America.

It's an ugly problem to deal with. Police officers see firsthand the devastating human suffering and injury resulting from these assaults—the broken bones, blackened eyes, bloodied faces, knife and gunshot wounds, and body bruises. We see the frustration and anguish suffered by battered women who are repeatedly assaulted and cannot find a safe refuge for themselves and their children anywhere in their community. We are well aware of the repetitive cycle of the abuse syndrome. Experience teaches us that if we are called to intervene in a domestic quarrel two or three times, that family will probably become one of our "regular customers." We also understand the increasing severity of each abuse incident—the slap which leads to a shove which leads to a punch which leads to a deadly assault.

We see, as few others do, the fear and bewilderment of the children who witness or become victims of these assaults. Often, as these children grow up, we encounter them as delinquents, prostitutes, runaways, or drug abusers.

As police officers, we know the enormous financial drain that domestic violence places on our resources. Domestic-related calls for help represent anywhere from fifteen to twenty-five percent of the workload of many urban police agencies, and one-third of all such calls involve quarrels where force has been or is being used. Moreover, *each* domestic call usually requires two or more police officers to spend anywhere from forty-five minutes to one hour in the home.

All too often, domestic violence leads to the death or serious injury of the responding officers. In an average year, thirty-two percent of assaults on police officers and sixteen percent of all police officers' deaths occur while handling domestic disturbance calls.

These dangerous domestic violence calls involve criminal behavior of the most serious nature: homicide, aggravated assault, assault with intent to kill, rape, battery, and terroristic threats. I am talking primarily about the use of hands and fists, but sometimes firearms and knives are used as well. It's a crime problem that threatens the survival of our family structure and impairs the social fabric of every community in this nation. It is a leading cause of divorce and a major contributing factor in juvenile delinquency and adult criminal behavior.

Experience has taught me to regard spouse abusers as habitual, hardcore offenders who almost invariably deny responsibility for their acts and blame their victims for the violence. Until recently, these people have enjoyed immunity from public censure because their crimes were committed behind closed doors in the sanctity of their homes. They also felt protected by the remnants of our legal tradition, which once expressly endorsed the right of a husband to inflict physical punishment on his wife, as well as by our social customs which have regarded spousal assaults as private family matters to be resolved without outside intervention. Offenders have also felt free to continue their violent acts because of the failure of any social institution, other than the police, to respond to the problem in a serious and consistent manner.

Fortunately, times are changing. Since 1976, nearly every state in the union has enacted legislation aimed at reducing domestic violence. South Carolina did so in 1984. In addition to providing much-needed funding for battered women's shelters, many statutes have authorized courts to issue protection orders as civil injunctions against future violence and have expanded police authority to make warrantless misdemeanor arrests when domestic violence is involved.

This expansion of police authority is a critical step in preventing further abuse. By arresting more abusers, police officers are sending a signal to everyone—onlookers and bystanders as well as offenders—that the abuser has committed a crime, that the victim has a right not to be beaten, and that the criminal justice system will take action, such as a jail term or court-supervised treatment for abusers, to stop the violence.

We know from a recent Police Foundation study of Minneapolis police responses to domestic violence that arrests *do* reduce subsequent acts of violence. The study found that arrest was twice as effective as mediation or separation of the parties in reducing repeated acts of violence. Similar studies are being carried out in several cities around the country.

It is absolutely unacceptable for the police to stand by and act only after someone has been beaten, raped, or killed. I believe arrests should be mandatory in all cases involving serious injury, the use or threatened use of a weapon, or violation of a protection order. Furthermore, I believe arrests are advisable in cases involving a newly committed misdemeanor assault, or in which the safety of the victim is in imminent danger. Unfortunately, not every police department in our state has taken advantage of this increased capability to assist victims.

Equal in importance to expanded arrest authority is the creation or expansion of battered women's shelters in our communities. Victims must have immediate access to safe shelter and protection from further abuse. They must be given an opportunity to receive emotional support, legal information, and counseling about available jobs, housing, and child care. As a police officer, I know of no greater frustration than responding to a domestic violence call and knowing that, if I cannot get the woman to a safe place, she will be beaten again as soon as her partner posts bail or returns from a "cooling-off" walk around the block.

While there have been many statutory changes and new programs started during the past decade, we have barely scratched the surface in addressing the problem of domestic violence. On behalf of battered women and their children, and on behalf of police officers who risk their lives every day to answer their calls for help, we need to provide the necessary resources and assistance that will put a stop to this intolerable situation.

The elderly are another group requiring special protection. The state of South Carolina has recently enacted legislation to protect the elderly from abuse and life-threatening neglect. It is now possible for law enforcement officers to take into protective custody any elderly person if an officer has reason to believe that this person is ill, abused, or in life-threatening danger. That officer must deliver the individual to a hospital or state social service agency for evaluation, treatment, and support.

A recent case in Charleston highlighted the need for the police to have authority of this kind. It was reported that an elderly woman was without food, seriously ill, and living in horrible conditions, neglected and abused by her own son who stole her welfare checks and frequently beat her when she complained.

Police officers found the woman suffering from open sores and bruises, which obviously were caused by a severe beating. There was no food in the house. The heating system had been disconnected. The woman was in bed, ill, unable to move, and lying in her own filth.

Too often in the past the police response to incidents of this kind has been, "There is nothing we can do." Now, in South Carolina, officers can act under the protection of state law without encountering civil liability. The woman was removed from the residence by ambulance despite the protests of her son, who already was responsible for systematically robbing, beating, and abusing her. She received medical treatment and is now living in a safe, secure, and caring environment—away from her son and free of his influence.

If police departments continue to insist that there is nothing they can do, then spouse abuse and abuse of the elderly will continue. I am convinced that the best remedy is to arrest the participants in family quarrels or brawls. If they know such conduct will result in arrest, the inconvenience and humiliation will cause them to think twice before repeating their performance, even if no jail sentence is imposed.

That's our policy in Charleston today. Don't lecture them, don't scold them, don't reason with them. Arrest them! Arrest them with their friends and neighbors looking on. You will be doing the neighborhood a favor. And you may well be preventing a homicide later on.

12
The Deadly American
Handgun

If a burglar breaks into your home at night and you
have a gun in the bedroom, it is foolhardy—madness,
really—to go about the house trying to confront him.
The burglar knows where you are likely to be at three
in the morning: in your bedroom asleep. But you don't
know where the burglar is, or how many intruders there
may be, or how they are armed. Even worse, if you
leave your bedroom you are momentarily framed in
the doorway, presenting any armed intruder with a
target almost impossible to miss. It is far better to call
the police on your bedroom telephone and ask for help.
Until it comes, stay in your bedroom. If the intruder
tries to come in, *he* will be framed in the doorway,
offering *you* a target that is difficult to miss.

Seeking a confrontation with an intruder under such
circumstances presumes that you are going to be able
to overcome him in some fashion. But suppose, as is
often the case, he overcomes you before you can shoot

him? Suppose he manages to put a bullet in you? Unless the police have been called, who will then protect your family? Or rescue you as you lie bleeding—perhaps bleeding to death—on the floor?

The impulse to seek out a burglar in the dark and challenge or capture him may have made some sense years ago when no telephones or other forms of assistance were available. But today it is just plain stupid. Unlike the daytime burglar who expects to find no one at home and most often will run if he does, the nighttime or "cat" burglar is a very dangerous creature who expects people to be at home and is prepared in advance to kill or seriously injure anyone who gets in his way. Most homeowners are no match for such a criminal. Even if by luck or chance the armed householder manages to surprise the intruder, he is not conditioned psychologically to shoot anyone, even a burglar, even in self-defense. Almost certainly he will hesitate, and such hesitation may cost him his life because the cat burglar will have no such scruples.

Knowing that I keep my service revolver loaded and close at hand at all times, a friend asked me, "What would you do if you woke up late at night and heard the sound of a prowler in the house?"

I said, "The first thing I'd do would be to reach out and touch my wife, to make sure that she hadn't decided to go to the kitchen for a glass of milk or something. We live alone, so I wouldn't have to worry about anyone else. Then I'd pick up the phone and dial 911. When the dispatcher answered, I would say, 'This is Chief Greenberg; you know my address. I think someone has broken into the house. I intend to remain in the bedroom. Send help, and be sure to tell the officers to identify themselves plainly when they arrive. I'll watch for the patrol car.'"

In less than five minutes police officers would be at

the door. If the burglar was still around, probably they'd capture him. This is the way to handle a situation like that. Don't try to be a hero. Call the cops—and sit tight.

Of course it's possible that the intruder may cut the telephone wire; burglars have been known to take this precaution. In that case, obviously, you won't be able to dial 911 or any other number. But a dead phone line can give you valuable information. It confirms your suspicion that someone has indeed entered your home. It is also a warning that you may well be in a life-or-death situation: if a criminal is *that* intent on isolating you, he probably will not hesitate to try to kill you if you interfere with him. The best response to a dead telephone is to lock the bedroom door and, if you are armed, shoot anyone who tries to break through it. If you are not armed, just be quiet and hope the intruder will take what he wants and go away. No possession, however valuable, is as valuable as your life.

No doubt, even in a situation like this, the knee-jerk reaction of some American males will be to seize their trusty six-shooter from the bedside table, or their faithful twelve-gauge from the closet, and go blundering out of the relative safety of the bedroom to confront or subdue the rascal who has violated the sanctity of their home. Don't make this mistake. The newspaper may call you a hero—but chances are you will be a dead hero. Your best line of defense is the telephone. If it's working, use it!

Almost invariably, handgun owners will tell you that they keep their weapon to repel burglars, pointing to the ever-increasing numbers of robberies reported by the press as justification. But burglars rarely intrude into premises that they believe to be occupied. The vast majority of residential burglaries are committed during daylight hours, or at other times when residents are not at home. More often than not, the burglar finds the handgun and adds it to his other loot. Now the gun owner has provided the criminal with a weapon that cannot be traced to that criminal and may well cause a death in some later holdup or robbery.

It is true that now and then newspapers carry an account of an episode where a homeowner armed with a handgun successfully protected himself and his family. But for every such case, those same news services will report hundreds of others where handgun owners have killed loved one, friends, or neighbors, sometimes in a fit of rage, sometimes in a tragic accident resulting from mistaken identity.

I have seen many cases in which a person owning a handgun, ostensibly to protect his family from robbers, rapists, kidnappers, and other criminals, has come to regret it bitterly. A few years ago I was called to the scene of a shooting where a fifteen-year-old boy lay dead on the living room floor. He had been shot twice in the chest. Apparently his father was awakened late at night by the sound of a window being raised downstairs. Thinking a burglar was in the house, he got up, took his revolver, and crept down to the living room. He saw a shadow duck behind a couch near the open window. He told us later that he called out several times, "Who's there?" Perhaps he did, maybe he didn't. In any case, getting no response, he fired six times into the couch. When nothing moved, he flicked on the lights and saw his son lying dead with a bullet through his heart. The boy had slipped out of the house after midnight to meet some friends. Coming back, he had found himself locked out, tried to enter through the window, and awakened his father.

A few days later I was called back to that same house. Again, a fatal shooting. Again, the victim was no burglar. This time it was the father. Unable to live with the knowledge that he had killed his own son, he had taken another handgun that he kept in the house and committed suicide. Here were two handguns, each purchased to protect the family from intruders, and here were two senseless and tragic deaths.

Another cause of household homicide is accidental death resulting from careless or improper storage of a handgun in a household with small children. I encountered a case recently where the owner had kept a pistol for several years on a high closet shelf, supposedly out of reach of the children. Eventually the children grew old enough to reach the gun with the aid of a chair, and one day they began playing with it. Moments later a shot rang out; one child had killed another. You may be sure that for the rest of his life the owner of that handgun will anguish over having brought it into his home.

In recent years there has been a great deal of debate about the wisdom of having a gun in the house. I'm not talking about shotguns or rifles used for hunting. I'm talking about handguns. Most experts who have studied the matter have concluded that handguns represent more danger to their owners and their owners' families than they do to any criminal intruder.

For the most part these experts are not inclined to jump on the gun control bandwagon. They know that there are far too many guns of all kinds in this country for any serious consideration to be given to banning gun ownership outright. We have waited too long; we are at least a century too late. There are simply too many weapons out there. There are some fifty-five to sixty million handguns in the United States today, with well over two million being added every year. This means that if we are to reduce significantly the number of Americans who own handguns, there will have to be a significant change in the wishes and attitudes of a great many individual citizens.

I might add that the dangers of handguns in the home do not apply to handguns kept at a place of business. When businesspeople keep guns at their establishments, especially small retail businesses, and those guns are used, it is almost always for the purpose for which they were purchased: to protect the business and to resist burglars and armed robbers. The last thing a businessperson wants to do is shoot a customer. Or an employee. As a result, guns held in such places rarely are involved in accidents or used irresponsibly.

Firearms of all kinds have a strange attraction for millions of Americans. Perhaps it goes back to frontier days when a gun was just about the most important single possession a man owned. First for hunting; survival often depended on it. Next for self-defense. In the early days of the Republic, guns were considered a guarantee of freedom from tyranny. "The right of the people to keep and bear arms," says the Constitution, "shall not be infringed."

Many of these historic reasons for Americans' love affair with guns have disappeared, but in countless Western movies the association of handguns with the good guys as well as the bad guys has left its mark, and guns play a major role in the current of violence that still sweeps through our movies today. Skilled marksmen have always been much admired, from Davy Crockett to Sergeant York.

All these influences are at work in the minds of people who have to make a key decision: whether or not private ownership of a firearm is in their own best interest.

There's no doubt about it, handguns kill a lot of

people in this country. I've heard it said—and I believe it's probably true—that more people are shot with handguns in the United States in a day than in Japan in a year. But you can't blame this entirely on the availability of guns. You have to take into consideration Americans' cultural conditioning about guns, the tendency of some to resort to violence to settle disputes, their lack of respect for rules of law or even for the sanctity of human life.

In these areas we have a long way to go before we find the answers.

One thing is certain: we won't find them by manufacturing and selling more than two million *additional* handguns every year.

13

In the Enemy's Camp

In a war, I've been told, if you're a general it helps to know what opposing commanders are like. If you know their background, their temperament, and how they react in given situations, your chances of defeating them are enhanced.

Likewise, if you're a law enforcement officer, it helps to know what your adversaries are like and what they're thinking. The more the members of a police force know about the mental and emotional makeup of the criminals they are supposed to control, the better their chances of success.

This is a relatively recent approach to crime control. For decades—for generations, really—police officers gave little thought to such things. They tried to control crime simply by arresting criminals. What the crooks were like didn't matter much; they were malevolent misfits; they were the enemy. The average cop was inclined to think that the average crook was pretty dumb.

If he wasn't dumb, why would he be a crook?

I was fortunate in coming to police work with a strong academic background in anthropology. The problem of conflict in human society always had fascinated me, because I saw that we all live in a world of conflict, not just military wars but social conflicts of every kind. Why are Catholics and Protestants at each other's throats in Northern Ireland? Why do Arabs clash endlessly with Jews? Why does conflict run so deep between blacks and whites? Even to begin to answer such questions, I had to study how human nature works and how human beings interact with one another. It's a field where ignorance usually prevails over enlightenment.

Take this assumption that most criminals are not very bright. As the song says, it ain't necessarily so. Even your average petty thief has the capacity to make quick decisions and act upon them. If you believe that the teenage purse snatcher is too stupid, too poorly educated, too warped by his environment to think clearly and logically—and fast— you are probably wrong.

Here's a little street scene that happened here in Charleston not long ago. Street thugs are breaking into parked cars using a simple but effective smash-grab-run technique. Police have planted a decoy car, locked but with valuables plainly visible. The officers are watching from a hiding place. A young thief approaches with a hammer hidden under his coat.

At this point a traffic officer who has not been briefed on the decoy operation happens to drive up in his marked police car. He parks a few yards away and begins to write out a report. The concealed officers reach for their radio to alert him and urge him to leave. But before they can make radio contact, the robber takes out his hammer, and within plain sight and sound of the police car, smashes the window, grabs the loot, and tries to run. The hidden officers emerge, of course, and seize him. Then they ask, "Why did you try to break into that car with a policeman in a patrol car not fifteen yards away? Didn't you see him?

Sure, the prisoner says, I saw him. But the presence of the patrol car convinced him that he was not getting into a decoy situation. He also made a quick estimate of the age of the officer: forty plus, too old to run down a seventeen-year-old thief. He figured, furthermore, that no passerby would try to interfere with him as he ran; surprise and fear would prevent it. The odds seemed to be in his favor. The rewards seemed greater than the risk. He made those calculations in a flash, and ninety-nine times out of a hundred they would have been valid. It wasn't stupidity on the criminal's part that caused his arrest. It was (from his point of view) bad luck. The logic of this particular smash-and-grabber was unassailable. It was the unforeseen element of chance that did him in.

Of course, the ability of crooks to think fast doesn't change the unyielding fact that they think differently from the rest of us. Stealing is not a question of right or wrong for most of these people; it's a way of life. Often in the ghetto—to use that overworked term—to be a successful thief is to command respect. Just as the gypsies over the centuries have supposedly prided themselves on stealing anything they wanted, especially horses, so the ghetto criminal regards effective thievery as a badge of merit. He generally looks down on honest wage earners with a mixture of amusement and contempt.

Suppose there are two cousins. One works hard as a stevedore for good wages and good benefits. The other looks for a job where there are opportunities to steal. Let's say he finds employment in a fancy hotel as a bellhop, his chances to steal are splendid. He sees a woman leave her purse unattended for a couple of minutes. With one quick swoop he opens it. In the purse is fifty dollars in cash, but he only takes twenty. He figures that if the woman misses it—by no means certain—she will think she lost it somehow. If it had been stolen, the thief would have taken all the money, right? Anyway, she's not likely to accuse a member of the hotel staff.

Or our larcenous bellhop, going down a corridor, sees through an open door a camera lying on a bed. So he walks into the room. If someone is there, he asks cheerfully if they called for a bellhop. If not, the camera goes into his pocket or under his jacket. He figures the victim will think one of the maids took it.

It's the same with the guy who parks the car. In some of them there will be valuables in the dashboard compartment: an electric door opener, a useful flashlight, something. If he is accused of taking them, he can always say he accidentally left the car unlocked. Someone came in and stole these items. Terribly sorry.

Meanwhile, the bellhop compares himself with his stevedore cousin, a comparison he makes with great satisfaction. There is that poor fellow paying income taxes, working like a dog in the hot sun in dirty clothes, straining his muscles, subject to periodic layoffs, without much chance to steal anything. How can that existence compare with his cousin's, who wears a nice uniform supplied by the hotel, works in air-conditioned comfort, pays little or no taxes, and if bored can always look for loose change that has fallen behind the sofa cushions or into chair linings in the lobby? The hotel owner is not going to ruin any upholstery to retrieve a few coins. But a bellhop with a razor blade has no such scruples. If that's not too productive, he can always shove a plastic bag or some such object into the coin-return passages of the pay telephones in the lobby, wait for a couple of days, then pull out the obstruction and hope for a shower of silver. If his conscience smites him—not likely—he can console himself that he's not stealing from the telephone company but from its customers. They may get mad at the operator for her failure to return their coins after an incomplete call. But so what? Whoever said that life is fair?

Stealing can become deeply ingrained in such people. I remember one young man—let's call him Marvin— who told me he needed a job. I felt sorry for him and, out of the goodness of my heart, I got him a job with a large automobile dealership. It was a pretty good job; all he had to do was drive cars back and forth between dealer and customer. Never get his hands dirty. No heavy work. Had a chance to work his way up to a better job.

Marvin went to work on Monday. On Friday—which was payday—he didn't show up. Or on the following Monday, or on Tuesday. His employer called me in some puzzlement: Where was Marvin? Was he sick? Why didn't he call in? I said I would come around to discuss the problem.

I asked the dealer some questions. Had Marvin complained about anything? No. Did he get along with the other employees? Seemed to. Was anything missing from the premises? Well, matter of fact, a box of tools was missing, probably worth sixty or seventy dollars. But this was nothing new. The dealer was used to having tools disappear. They vanished all the time.

I went around to Marvin's house where he lived with several brothers and sisters in far from opulent surroundings. I asked Marvin if he was sick, No. Why, then, was he not at work? Pause. Frown. People didn't like him at that place. Had he had a disagreement with his supervisor? No. Had anyone been unkind to him?

No. But they didn't like him. That's why he wasn't working? A blank stare.

I brought up the subject of the missing tools. Had he taken them? No. Was he *sure* he hadn't taken them? Firm denial. But I knew he was lying, and after some persistent questioning Marvin admitted he had stolen the tools.

Now comes the interesting question: Why? The value of the tools was nothing compared to the value of the job, at which Marvin could have been making more money than the rest of his family combined. Marvin didn't know why—but I did. It was because he had never had a job that lasted. No one in the family had ever had a job that lasted. So why should this one last? It wouldn't, so he might as well take the opportunity to steal something while it did last.

That was pure ghetto logic. Indeed, there is always some kind of logic to life in the ghetto, even when it seems twisted to us. I knew one young Casanova who had a girlfriend whom he liked very much. In fact, he said he loved her. But when they had sex, he never used a contraceptive.

"Why not?" I asked him. "You carry one right there in your wallet, don't you?"

Yes, he did, but this was for tramps or one-night stands or casual sex encounters. He didn't want any of those women getting pregnant and having a kid by him. He'd be ashamed of that. He didn't want his girlfriend to get pregnant either, but if she did, that was all right because she wasn't a tramp. Logic again. Of sorts.

I remember another young man who came to work as a trainee in a supermarket where I worked part-time on the security end of things. This young fellow had a bit of a criminal record, but now, we were assured by social workers and other angels of mercy, he was completely reformed and hence completely reliable.

In time his training brought him to the checkout line, where he seemed bright and alert and had nimble fingers when it came to ringing up sales as the customers came past with their baskets of groceries. Trouble was, on the second day, a whole set of new customers appeared, all relatives of our checkout wizard—his sisters and his cousins and his aunts. As they came through the line he rang up their purchases, but he reduced the price of each item by about eighty percent. So the customer had a sales slip all right, but the total on it was eighty percent too low.

I nailed this fellow easily by watching him from a concealed place with a pair of binoculars, which enabled me actually to see the discrepancies as he rang them up on the register. But even when retribution followed, I'm sure his expertise in defrauding the supermarket was regarded with tolerance if not downright admiration in the circles in which he moved. Logically, why not? He was feeding the whole community, wasn't he?

Many middle-class people misunderstand or misinterpret things they see in the ghetto. Perhaps they see a weather-beaten shack, so run down that it seems to be pondering which way to fall. Obviously, very low-income people live there. But parked outside is a late-model Cadillac. Is this the property of the shack dweller? Yes, it is. He's buying it on credit, of course, but he's the legal owner.

What sort of madness is this? How can one account for it? Very easily, if one understands the dynamics of ghetto life and ghetto thinking. That car is there because of its symbolic value to the owner of the shack. He knows that in terms of housing or club memberships he will never be able to compete with the vice-president of the company, or the owner of the factory where he works. So he doesn't try. But in terms of *wheels*, he can be their equal or perhaps even their superior. That's an American yardstick that everyone can understand. It says, Hey, look, I may not have fancy clothes and I don't eat in fancy restaurants, but I have a fancy car, and I'm going to drive it as long as I can make the payments. That's why that car is sitting outside that shack. It's an ego prop for someone whose ego has nothing else to support it.

The other day I went into a poor home, very poor indeed. Cracked linoleum on the floor, torn wallpaper on the walls, broken-down sofa in the living room. But on a table beside the sofa was a brand-new telephone answering machine. Here again, a symbol of impor- tance, even though all the other symbols said "poverty." The machine cost eighty or ninety dollars. No matter. It said to the owner, If someone calls, you can record what they say. That's important. Maybe it's your boss telling you to report, maybe it's your girlfriend who's dying to see you. Those things are important, and if important things are happening in your house, *you're* important, a yearning common to all of us, criminals and noncriminals alike.

The more closely you look at human nature, the more complex the whole question of crime and punishment becomes. You may have three or four individuals in- volved in the commission of a single crime, and all may have different motives for committing it. Take a hypothetical case like this one. Actually, it's not entirely hypothetical because grisly replicas of it take place with depressing frequency in the grimier sections of some of our cities.

In this crime, four young hoodlums decide to rob an old man drowsing on a bench in a deserted park. The skin-color of the hoods doesn't matter; they could be white, yellow or black, but all are probably the same color. They have met at some playground, perhaps, and have roamed off in a pack, looking for excitement, looking for trouble, looking for money. They see the old man and decide he's a promising target. They beat him and rob him, and when he doesn't have enough money to placate them, they douse him with gasoline or kerosene or lighter fluid and set him on fire.

Now who are these charming people? The oldest one, about sixteen, comes from a higher income stratum than the others. His mother has a good government job; his father is a dentist. But they don't have much time for him. He finds nothing emotionally satisfying at home, but he fancies himself the leader of this minigang, and there are satisfactions in that. He's anxious to show how tough and macho he can be.

The second mugger, a bit younger, comes from a very poor family. His motive is simple and direct: money. He figures if the old man has thirty or forty dollars on him, his share of it will make the robbery worth the risk. When the old man doesn't have that kind of money, his reaction is rage. Ordinarily, beating the victim might suffice, but this time he is willing to go along with the plan to turn the old man into a flaming torch.

This idea comes from the third mugger, and he is the one who actually tosses the match. For whatever reason, he is someone who enjoys inflicting pain. Where did this sadistic streak come from? Who knows? Perhaps as a baby he was beaten and abused. Perhaps as a small boy he enjoyed stamping on anthills or tormenting kittens. He knows right from wrong. If a blue uniform comes around the corner he will flee instantly, as will all the others. But this is of little consolation to the old man.

The fourth member of the group, the youngest, would never initiate such an action by himself. Perhaps secretly he deplores it, and wishes it would stop. But peer pressure is a powerful influence; he is actually afraid to voice any objection, or even to run away, so he stands there helplessly, as guilty in the eyes of the law as the others are.

Unless the police are summoned immediately, there's not much chance for the old man. There's not a very good chance of apprehending the criminals either, unless some witness is able to give a description of them and point out which way they ran. Even if they are all captured, the fact that they are juveniles will make prosecution difficult. And if they're convicted, wouldn't it take a latter-day Solomon to decide what the punishment in each case should be? Should consideration be given to the fact that the leader had an unhappy home environment? Or that poverty was a factor in the second mugger's decision to participate? Or that the sadistic member of the gang never received psychiatric counseling? Or the fact that the least culpable member nevertheless took his share of the stolen money and offered no word of protest as the flames engulfed the old man?

Human motivation is so complex that it almost defies analysis. Clearly, in a case like this—or almost any case—criminals participating in the same crime do so for a variety of individual reasons. But there is one common denominator that stands out clearly, and that is the element of choice. Nobody compelled any of these young hoodlums to rob and burn the old man. They made a conscious decision to do so. If you cannot accept this concept of free choice, then the whole notion of accountability goes out the window, and with it a large section of the foundation on which society ultimately rests.

Deep and wide in law enforcement circles is the chasm between those who accept this concept of choice and accountability and those who do not. In 1985, Simon & Schuster published a book by James Q. Wilson and Richard J. Herrnstein titled *Crime and Human Nature*. It turned out to be a very controversial book.

The authors suggest that the decision to engage in criminal activity is formulated on essentially the same basis as any other decision people make—they choose it because they prefer it. A person's behavior, it is argued, is determined by an assessment of the consequences of that behavior, or as the writers put it, "A person will do that thing the consequences of which are perceived by him to be preferable to the consequences of doing something else."

Crime, then, becomes a by-product of an individual's particular method of obtaining some desired goal. If a person prefers to obtain that goal immediately and is willing to discount or chance the risks of acting on impulse, he is much more likely to commit a crime than those who realize that most of life's worthwhile goals require some degree of significant effort and some delay in obtaining them.

Unfortunately (to my way of thinking), a whole industry has been developed in this country to support the theory that crime is not the result of a choice that an individual makes, but is the consequence primarily of medical, environmental, social, and psychological processes from which the criminal cannot escape. Therefore it is these processes that must be dealt with, not the individual, who, it is argued, is basically blameless.

The theory put forward by Wilson and Herrnstein, I believe, is the one with the most merit. The theory of choice alone can explain how and why it is that persons from almost identical backgrounds can react to opportunities for crime in such markedly different ways. There is much opposition to this theory, especially in academic circles. But I believe that most of us in law enforcement whose role it is to locate, arrest, and deter criminals would say that the central theory of the book was derived from common sense and is supported by the experiences of police officers in their contacts with criminals elsewhere.

I would say further that when a police force bases its thinking and actions on the attitude that society's enemies make free choices about their behavior, crime deterrence takes on a sharp and effective focus designed to change not only what a criminal thinks about crime, but what he does about a crime opportunity.

We've supplied that attitude here in Charleston.

We've found that it works.

14
Making Crooks Miserable

The mental processes of habitual crooks never fail to amaze and fascinate me. Let's consider a typical case.

Having obtained a gun somewhere—no great trick in our society—a teenager decides to rob a convenience store. Usually—but not always—he waits until darkness falls. Sometimes—but not always—he tries to conceal his features with a ski mask or a stocking mask. He holds the gun on the proprietor, makes him open the cash register, scoops up whatever money may be there, and takes off into the night.

What does he gain? A hundred dollars or so. Maybe less. What does he risk? A lot.

If he's caught and convicted, he may spend the next few years in jail. Is the gain—a hundred dollars—worth that kind of risk? Not to any realist.

If the proprietor of the store has a gun and knows how to use it, the robber may wind up in the city morgue. Is the gain worth the risk? Not to any rational person.

And yet, there's an epidemic of such robberies in just about every city in the land. How to account for it?

To find a reason that makes sense you have to look inside the robber's head. In particular, you have to ask yourself how he views the future. The answer to this question is that he *doesn't* view the future. He doesn't think about tomorrow at all. He considers only his needs for today. If stealing a hundred dollars or fifty dollars will satisfy those needs, then from his point of view his actions make perfectly good sense.

According to Harvard sociologist Edward Banfield, a petty thief like this lives a life hemmed in by a "narrow time horizon" in which only the present counts. There are literally thousands of these street thugs in our society doing a tremendous amount of damage, not just monetary damage, but psychological damage as well. A handful of street toughs allowed to roam unchecked, snatching purses, breaking into automobiles, and mugging elderly citizens will do more to degrade a community's character than more sophisticated crooks robbing a local bank of many thousands of dollars. By and large, honest citizens are not afraid of bank robbers. But they are terrified of the lurking shadow in the streets at night.

Another curious aspect of the criminal mind-set—and this one is known to every policeman—is the crook's attitude toward property. If a pickpocket steals your wallet and puts it in his own pocket, does he consider that money to be yours? Not at all. Now it's *his* money, and he will fight you tooth and nail to keep it. Burglars have the same attitude. Once they lay hold of it, that TV set, that microwave oven, that gold necklace isn't yours anymore. It's theirs. Theirs to keep, to fence, to pawn or sell. Great is their indignation if some other crook tries to take it from them. But their concept of property rights is a current that flows only one way—toward themselves.

Who can say where this attitude originates? Perhaps it's a reflection of the welfare environment in which most of these petty criminals grow up, an environment where payments are made and benefits flow from some invisible and apparently inexhaustible source. If those payments and benefits "belong" to the recipients without any effort on their part, perhaps it is no great leap to the conclusion that anything they want or "need" belongs to them and they have a right to take it.

I think it's likely, too, that some of these street toughs are affected, consciously or unconsciously, by the arguments of those who claim that a criminal's offenses are not his fault. The poor fellow, they say, is just expressing anger and resentment against a cruel world. The real culprit is society.

The do-gooders are convinced that the real culprit is the family that didn't provide him with a proper upbringing.

The school that didn't teach him to read.

The church that failed to provide ethical guidance.

The television programs that depict his ethnic group in menial roles.

The job market that will not let him in.

The political system that refuses him participation.

These are the things, it is argued, that need to be changed, rather than the person who robbed, beat, and raped an elderly widow. That person doesn't need punishment; he needs "treatment."

Your average crook eagerly embraces the notion that he needs treatment. Treatment is the briar patch where the prison inmate is happiest, because he knows that the underlying purpose of treatment is to get him out of jail sooner. In recent years, a whole rehabilitative industry has sprung up in our correctional facilities. The criminals soon learn the language, thoughts, and theories of this industry. They almost never refuse to participate in treatment programs because they know very well how to use them. They pretend to be reformed. They play along until they are released with a shortened sentence or an early parole. Then they turn and laugh at the institution that is supposed to have rehabilitated them.

Well, you may say, it's not the police officer's function to judge such things. Maybe not, but the police officer is the one who must cope with the results and clean up the mess. Our primary mission as law-enforcers may be to arrest law-breakers after a crime has been committed and put them in jail. But if we assume—as I do—that a crook is a crook by choice, then we cops also have a responsibility to try to influence that choice. Influence it in a negative way whenever possible, so that instead of choosing to commit the crime, he chooses *not* to do so.

Negative persuasion is a policy we apply constantly in Charleston. It involves making known criminals as unhappy and uncomfortable as possible in the hope they will decide that carrying out an illegal act in Charleston is too hazardous, the risks too great, the probable rewards too meager. We hope that certain measures will cause them to choose *not* to commit a crime. Or if they simply must commit one, they will do it elsewhere.

One such measure we call confrontation. The criminal element in most places is made up of only a fraction of the population, and in most towns the police officers know very well who these people are. If they see Johnny the burglar walking down the street with an innocent look on his face and a tire iron in his hand, they are probably quite justified in assuming that he is not on his way to help some stranded motorist.

The foot patrolman on that street has a perfect right to go up and speak to Johnny. He may phrase it in a variety of ways, but his basic message is this: Get off my beat! I don't want to see you around here again. I know who you are and I know what you do. I think I know what you have in mind and I don't like it. If you stay around here, I'll do my best to get you for littering or jaywalking or something. So get lost!

Very likely Johnny will choose another part of Charleston for his strolls, or with luck another town altogether.

Is this a form of harassment? Not at all. A cat may look at a king. A cop may speak to a known criminal.

Confrontation is a skill—it's almost an art—that good cops master quickly. Let's say I'm driving down the street in civilian clothes, and I see a man walking along carrying a paper bag and looking in store windows. Some instinct in me warns me he's casing the stores. He's not just window-shopping. Which stores look easy to break into? Which ones have merchandise that can be carried away easily? Which ones have effective locks or burglar alarms? And so on.

So I stop the car and beckon him over. "Hi there, haven't I seen you around before?"

He doesn't think so.

"Well, how you doin', anyway?"

"Okay." He doesn't know I'm a cop, but he's wary.

"When did you get out?" No use asking him if he was in jail. He'll say he wasn't. But the question surprises him into telling the truth. He says he got out two weeks ago.

"What were you in for?" He says it had to do with drugs. The paper bag he's carrying might contain drugs, but I don't think so. More likely it contains one of the most effective of all burglar tools: a change of clothing. Suppose he tries to rob someone, or does rob someone. Suppose the victim dials 911 and gives a description of the thief. White T-shirt. Faded blue shorts. Dark glasses. Dirty yellow cap with splashes of paint on it. Pretty good description really. But give the guy twenty seconds in a dark alley or in the men's room of a service station, and suddenly there he is in a checked shirt and long brown corduroys. No dark glasses. No yellow cap—that's in the bin with the used paper towels in the men's room. He's smart enough to wear shorts for the robbery itself because it's easier to slip long pants over shorts than over another pair of pants. Oh, yes. A change of clothing is a burglar's best ally.

What do I do about my newfound friend? I can't arrest him; he hasn't committed a crime—not yet, anyway. I can't make him open his paper bag—no probable cause. So I pick up a camera I have lying on the car seat and point across the street. "Would you mind standing over there for just a moment? I want a picture of that building and I need a person in it to get the proportions right."

Maybe he won't cooperate. But maybe he will; most of us like to have our pictures taken. But whether he likes it or not . . . click! There he is on film. Now if he robs someone and the victim comes to us, we'll have his face on film for the victim to identify down at the jail.

Confrontation can take many forms. In Charleston, if one of our foot patrolmen spots a known shoplifter in a store, he doesn't wait for the thief to steal something. He informs the shop owner in loud and unmistakable tones that the kid in the green T-shirt or the woman in the brown coat has a record of shoplifting, has been convicted of shoplifting in the past, and therefore may reasonably be expected to try to shoplift again. The grateful shopkeeper then fixes the individual with a baleful eye and watches him or her slink out of the store. The weapon being brought to bear here is shame. A crook may not mind *being* a crook, but it's embarrassing to have the truth proclaimed in public. He can't sue the patrolman for slander because he knows the statement is true. All he can do is vanish as quickly as possible.

Our foot patrolmen in Charleston are carefully chosen men who play a very important role in our war against crime. It's not like the old days when this assignment was considered a punishment. Remember how the irascible captain used to bawl to an offending detective? "One more goof out of you, Murphy, and you'll be back pounding a beat!"? That doesn't happen anymore.

Cops in a patrol car can only be aware of what they see through the windshield. They're really in a glass and steel cage. But the foot patrolman can see everything and hear everything and smell everything on his beat. In Charleston that beat is just three blocks long, no more. Three blocks in a straight line. No side streets, because a cop can't see around corners. A foot patrolman knows everyone on his beat who has a right to be there. He's a little suspicious of everyone else. A really good cop has kind of built-in radar that warns him when something is wrong. Even when he doesn't know what that something is, he doesn't just go home and forget about it. He keeps turning it over in his mind. He keeps chewing on it until he figures out what it is. This kind of cop is a bulldog. He never lets go. Now and then he may get into trouble for being a bit over-zealous, but he accepts the occasional reprimand philosophically. He figures it's part of his job. As a rule, our foot patrol cops serve two years on a given beat. The private citizens on that beat are very glad to have them there. The crooks are not.

We have another method of pressuring known criminals; we call it monitoring. We watch them, day and night. We follow them everywhere. We make no secret of it. We want them to know they're being watched and followed. It makes them very nervous, very unhappy. That is the object of the exercise. Is it expensive in terms of time and manpower? Yes, it is. But suppose the crook being followed is a known cat burglar, skilled and determined. Suppose in the past he has averaged four burglaries a week. If you can prevent him from attempting *any* burglaries, is the cost of watching him worth it? His potential victims would certainly say that it is. So will the city fathers, if they're wise.

Recently we have been experimenting with yet another procedure designed to bring alarm and despondency to the criminal classes. We call it a checkpoint. One of the best ways to discourage illegal enterprises is to go after the customers. That's what a checkpoint is designed to do. Usually we set up a checkpoint with no advance warning near some establishment where unsavory people gather: a tavern notorious for harboring drunken drivers, a bar where drug pushers hang out, a roadhouse where frequent stabbings or shootings occur.

A checkpoint has to be carefully planned. You don't want side streets where drivers who spot the trap can turn off and vanish. The intercepting team doesn't have to be very elaborate; a couple of motorcycle cops will do. Plus an officer with a handheld video camera. But there are backup patrol cars standing by, just out of sight, whose job it is to pursue any vehicle that makes a U-turn and tries to run for it.

Obviously, if someone tries to escape, he has a guilty conscience about something. Maybe he's driving with a suspended license. Maybe he knows he can't pass a sobriety test. Maybe he has cocaine or marijuana in the car. Maybe there's a warrant outstanding for his arrest on any one of a thousand charges.

Law-abiding drivers have nothing to fear. We check their driver's license and car registration and send them on their way. Minor offenders may be given a citation. But if a driver wrenches his car around and tries to run, a radio call goes out: "Red Mustang coming your way. Pick him up!" And the hidden patrol cars do just that. If the driver of the red Mustang tries to jettison drugs as he flees, the handheld video camera will provide us with evidence that he threw something, and usually it's easy to retrieve the drugs from the side of the road or wherever they landed.

Sometimes the net catches a big fish. Not long ago, after a furious chase, the driver of the fleeing car jumped out and ran into the woods. But we have faster cops—our Flying Squad—who ran him down. He turned out to be wanted for murder. He had been evading capture for months—until the checkpoint caught him. Flying Squad members can outfight, outrun, and outdistance any crook on the street. That's their job. In the Old West, they used to hire the fastest guns; we hire the fastest guys. Because the street thugs themselves are mostly between the ages of fifteen and twenty-five, we need officers in their twenties. And we issue them running shoes.

We have been staging these checkpoints for some time, and we plan to continue the procedure. When the word gets around, people will think twice before patronizing their sleazy old haunts. If enough customers stay away, the establishment will go out of business. Good riddance.

The police action that makes some crooks unhappiest is confiscation of the tools of their trade. A gambling ring, let's say has set up its headquarters in Charleston.

The operators are not too concerned about being arrested. Gambling is just a misdemeanor in most places. They figure they can post bond and be back in business in a couple of hours. Imagine their dismay and chagrin, then, when they come back to their snug headquarters and find the tables gone, the chairs gone, the telephones gone, the typewriters gone, maybe even the air conditioner window units gone—all seized as evidence of their illegal activities.

Where did everything go? Into a police van, that's where. And there this evidence will remain until the case is disposed of in court. Then perhaps a poor family's belongings will be stolen, or wiped out in a fire. Suddenly the police van will roll around and do what it can to replace their lost belongings. Now the good guy in the blue uniform has turned into Robin Hood, taking from the criminal rich and giving to the needy poor.

Is this really and truly legal? Absolutely. If it weren't we wouldn't do it.

15
Finding The Pressure Points

A lot of cops are convinced that the best solution to a crime is to make an arrest. They like to follow a nice, logical, standard procedure: observe the criminal in the act of committing a crime, apprehend him, bring him down to the jail, lock him up.

But there are limitations to this somewhat simplistic approach. It's not always possible to observe a robber in the act of robbing, or a rapist in the act of raping. In many cases where a crime has almost certainly occurred, there may not be enough evidence to justify an arrest. In other cases, an individual may not actually be breaking the law but nevertheless can be a definite nuisance or menace to those around him.

In such cases the solution may not lie in making an arrest at all, but in applying pressure in a way that will cause the offender to cease and desist from his undesirable activities. Figure out pressure points where the offender is vulnerable, and tighten the screws—sometimes psychological screws—until the desired results are obtained.

The first time I realized how effective this technique can be was in California, when I was working as a Human Relations officer in Berkeley. At the time, a motorcycle gang known as Hell's Angels was terrorizing a part of town. They had set up headquarters in a small restaurant owned by a timid soul who wished desperately that the Hell's Angels were where their name implied they belonged, or anywhere rather than in his little establishment. Technically the Angels weren't breaking any law. They were just rough and ugly, their language was coarse, the waitresses were afraid of them, and when they parked their big hulking "hogs" outside the restaurant's front door, customers stayed away in droves.

The conventional approach would have been to wait until the Angels hurt someone or did some physical damage to the premises, and then arrest them. But it was obvious that this might take some time. Nobody was ready to cross those thugs, so chances of an assault complaint were low. As for the premises, the proprietor was too afraid of them to utter a peep even if they broke all the chairs and tables in the place.

But even Hell's Angels have vulnerable areas. The trick was to apply increasing pressure to those areas. Not in any obvious or dramatic way. Just enough to make them move on to someplace else.

I figured the Angels had two pressure points. One was their bikes. With a motorcycle in view at all times, a member of the gang seemed ten feet tall. The gang liked this particular cafe because they could park their bikes right in front. That said to everyone, "The Hell's Angels are here—watch out!"

So we painted the curb yellow in front of the place. If the Angels parked there, they would get a parking ticket. Simple as that. Now they had to park their bikes in back, out of sight. That was pressure point number one.

The second pressure point had to do with the Angels' macho image. They were tough, they were hairy, they were mean, they wore black leather jackets glazed with dirt. You've probably known people who get upset if their surroundings are dingy and dirty. Well, there are also some characters who get upset if their surroundings are clean and sparkling.

So we persuaded the proprietor to close the place for three days. In those three days a kind of sanitary revolution took place. The walls were painted. The grease was scraped off the ceiling fans. Frilly curtains appeared at the windows. There were flowers in vases on the tables. The waitresses all wore demure little sexless uniforms; they looked like schoolmarms or librarians. When the Angels came back, they scowled and glared and stomped around for a while. Finally they went out back, jumped on their hogs, roared away, and never returned. No arrests. No confrontations. No fights. Just a little judicious pressure at the right places—the pressure points.

Sometimes a complex situation may have many pressure points. The most effective technique is to hit them all at once and hit them hard. When I came in as chief of police in the town of Opa Locka, Florida, cockfighting had been going on as long as anyone could remember.

Cockfighting is a barbaric practice in which human beings train cocks—or roosters, as they are usually called—to fight to the death. Actually, not much training is required; fighting cocks are naturally aggressive. If confined in pens in close proximity to one another, and then released in a pit or an enclosure with walls three or four feet high, they will fight furiously to establish dominance. Humans make these combats even more bloody by strapping long, razor-edged metal spurs onto the legs of the cocks, thereby rendering the fights more gory and vicious—and shorter.

There are no referees, no timeouts, and no humane considerations. The loser almost always dies. Sometimes both birds die. In the meantime, tens of thousands of dollars change hands. As always, where money is at stake, emotions run high. There are frequent disputes, often violent, and fights between humans as well as roosters often occur. Sticks, knives, and sometimes guns are used. These fights, too, may be fought to the death.

This bloody and brutal "sport" is a crime almost everywhere. It certainly was in Florida. Even so, it had been going on virtually undisturbed by the police for a number of years. There were rumors of payoffs, but a more likely reason was the frustration the police felt when they raided the cockfighting establishment and no effective prosecution or judicial action followed. Gambling was just a misdemeanor. Those arrested would bond themselves out within a couple of hours and be right back in the arena shouting and screaming and betting as wildly as ever. Cockfighting in Opa Locka was just another gambling activity that officials tolerated.

When a troubled citizen came to me complaining that his employees on the swing shift were unable to park their cars because of the cockfighting crowds, he also gave me a clue to the solution. He said rather bitterly that although he had to pay taxes and purchase a business license, the cockfighting enterprise did neither—and yet those people seemed to have more access to the streets than he did.

Business license! These illegal operations were businesses, and that was where the pressure points lay. I knew already that simple arrest was ineffective when it came to gambling, or any vice activity for that matter. In order to defeat them, we would have to attack the business itself.

I had already decided that I could not head up a department that many people thought was corrupt or ineffective or both. We were going to hit those criminals hard in a way that would do some permanent good. We would not try to make mass arrests. Indeed, we would make as few arrests as possible. We were going to attack the *business* of cockfighting by using the city's legislative and police powers in the broadest sense.

As I expected, the cockfight promoters indeed had not applied for a business license. A large arena with bleachers capable of seating approximately four hundred people had been constructed in the warehouse that housed the operation. The bleachers had been built without a permit, so they were in violation of the building code. Food, liquor, and cigarettes were sold, without health department approval—also in violation of code.

The violations of the various building codes would permit us to padlock the building and to order the water and electricity shut off. With so many people attending the cockfights and with so few exits, we were sure that the operation would not meet fire department standards, so we decided to ask the fire marshal to join in the raid.

We decided to hit the warehouse on Wednesday, the biggest night of the week, which would spread the word in a hurry about the new kind of crackdown that we were conducting. A final briefing was held the night of the raid. All participating groups were given their assignments. The key was surprise and a dominating show of strength. That way no one would be inclined to offer resistance. A phalanx of police officers would force their way in, and others would follow behind to their predetermined positions.

The fire inspectors were to count the number of persons in the warehouse and check for fire hazards.

The code enforcement officers would condemn the premises for being in violation of the building code and order all utilities cut off immediately.

The state liquor control agents would arrest the persons selling liquor without a license and confiscate all liquor, beer, and wine as well as two unlicensed cigarette machines.

The health department inspector would close down the snack bar and seize all food stocks.

The raid went off as planned. Complete surprise. Not a hitch.

When the crowd became aware that we intended to search everyone before allowing them to leave, the noise of guns being dropped on the floor sounded like thunder.

Computer checks on the crowd revealed a dozen or more individuals wanted on outstanding arrest warrants ranging from shoplifting and traffic offenses to armed robbery and burglary. The cops checking the cars in the parking lot turned up several stolen cars and numerous expired license tags, expired inspection stickers, and equipment violations.

Several drunk driving arrests were made as intoxicated participants attempted to drive off.

No one was arrested for resisting arrest or being disorderly. We had entered armed to the teeth, with sufficient numbers and such efficient organization that it was clear that there was no way that any resistance would succeed.

Meanwhile the city manager, Donald McKenna, had an ordinance drawn up forbidding anyone to organize, attend, or be present in any location where any animal, whether reptile, fowl, mammal, or insect, was caused to fight with any other animal or human being for the purpose of providing entertainment or exhibition of any kind.

This ordinance was introduced and passed in its first reading at the next city council meeting.

Any one of our various measures might not have been sufficient in itself to end the cockfighting. But together they added up to irresistible pressure from every conceivable governmental angle. Having so many different agencies involved ensured that attempts at bribery or payoffs could not succeed. Shutting off utilities and seizing the cocks presented instant obstacles to this illegal enterprise. (The cocks were turned over to the Humane Society.) The enforcement of building codes and zoning laws represented longer-term blocks. The most effective single action was an order from the fire marshal fixing an occupancy capacity of no more than forty-five people for that building. Even if all the other obstacles were overcome, there was simply no way that a cockfight could be profitable with so few spectators or bettors.

Screening automobile registrations, checking for arrest warrants, and picking up drunk drivers was also an extremely effective deterrent. The whole effort was wrapped up with the passing of the anti-cockfighting ordinance.

Every business has its pressure points. Cockfighting is a business—an illegal business. You undermine a business by attacking its suppliers, concessionaires, operators, employees, and customers.

Opa Locka has been free of cockfighting for over a decade.

16
Rehabilitation: The Great American Myth

A few chapters back I spoke of the huge rehabilitation industry that has grown up in and around our penal system in the last half century or so. It is made up of psychiatrists, psychologists, social workers, counselors, chaplains, and other optimists. At the heart of their work lies a belief that, as a society, we are smart enough to turn habitual criminals around so that when they are released from prison they will walk the straight and narrow path forevermore.

In my opinion, the system is a colossal failure. And the figures bear me out. Take burglars, for example. When they are released from prison, eighty-three percent of them are back in jail within two years—for the same offense.

Of course, the rehabilitationists and I part company right away. They say to the prisoner, "You are in prison so that we can reform you." I would say to the same prisoner, "You are in jail because you deserve to be punished."

There's a world of difference in those two attitudes. One says to the prisoner, You are here because of unfortunate circumstances, of deprivations in your background, of society's shortcomings. The other says, You are here because, exercising your God-given free will, you chose to commit certain antisocial acts, you were caught and convicted, and now you are being punished by isolating you from those whom you would victimize.

I offer no apologies when I say that I am all in favor of jails. One reason is that they offer real equity when it comes to punishing criminals. If you try to punish crooks with fines, that's instantly inequitable, because a given fine hurts a rich person much less than a poor person. But everyone—rich, poor, young, old—has exactly the same amount of time at his or her disposal. Therefore if you punish, say, two people by depriving them of the same amount of free time (which is what identical jail sentences theoretically do), then the punishment is the same in both cases.

Keeping felons in prison is one of the things we do best. Almost no prisoners try to escape, and even fewer succeed. I don't think jails should be medieval dungeons with slime on the walls and rats running around, but they could be a lot more Spartan than most of them are. If prisoners find themselves more restricted and less comfortable than they were before they were sentenced, so what? Why should we flinch from the notion of punishment inflicted simply as punishment?

The trouble is, to be an effective deterrent, punishment needs to be swift and certain, and in our society it almost never is. I have never forgotten a little old lady who was pointed out to me once during a visit to New York. She was about seventy, bent over, frail, carrying a shopping bag through one of the most crime-

ridden areas of the city. All the junkies and street hoodlums watched her go by, knowing that she probably
was carrying fifty or sixty thousand dollars in cash because she was a bag lady for the numbers racket. She
had no guards, no armored trucks, no police escort.
But no one touched her because everyone knew that
punishment for doing so would be immediate, drastic,
and final. No Miranda warnings, no lawyers, no delays,
no appeals. Just instant trouble, big trouble, terminal
trouble for anyone who laid a hand on the old lady.
So nobody did.

The widespread legal custom of granting probation
for a first offense—what's the point of that? It just gives
juvenile crooks a license to commit their first crime. If
they know there will be no punishment, that they have
what amounts to a guarantee of immunity for a first
offense, why should they hesitate?

Or consider the parole system, which is one of the
main devices for getting crooks out of overcrowded
jails. I was a parole officer once myself, in California.
I was paid to keep track of 150 parolees, watch them,
supervise them, check on them at least once a month.
It was ridiculous. I couldn't begin to do an adequate
job of supervision, let alone provide counseling or support. And I remember wondering, if these released
criminals couldn't be trusted and had to be watched,
why weren't they still in jail where it would have been
much easier to watch them? The main reason they
weren't was that there was no room for them there. I
truly believe that, if we had the jail space available, it
would probably make very good sense to abolish the
parole system altogether.

Speaking of parole reminds me of a sterling character
named Timothy Evans. By rights, a person with a name
like that should be a Welsh singer or an Irish poet. Mr.
Evans was neither. He was, however, a pretty good

example of how our criminal justice system works. Or usually doesn't work.

In 1980, here in Charleston, Timothy Evans beat, gagged, and raped two sisters who were in their eighties. He pleaded simple assault. The women were too traumatized and ashamed to testify. He got and served thirty days.

About a year and a half later, on the Fourth of July, a white woman of about fifty-five was returning to her apartment after a trip to the laundromat when she saw a shadowy figure lurking in some bushes along the street. She tried to run, but Timothy Evans pursued her and pounced on her from behind. She managed to shake him off and fled, screaming, but he caught her again near the door to her apartment, beat her in the face with his fists, flung her to the ground and began ripping off her clothing. Her screams were heard by another woman in the apartment house who opened her door, saw what was going on, and dialed 911. She gave our dispatcher a description of the assailant. Meanwhile, aware that his evening's recreation had been observed and reported, Timothy Evans released his victim and melted into the shadows.

When a call like that comes in and the exact location of the crime is known, it's our custom to send only one officer to the scene. Other officers fan out through the neighborhood in an effort to catch the criminal. All nearby units are alerted by radio. In this case an officer a few blocks away in a squad car saw an individual who matched the description of the assailant. When the officer tried to call him over, Timothy Evans took off like an antelope.

These young thugs can run—and run fast. Usually they choose an escape route through the backyards of houses where a squad car can't go. In this case the officer jumped from his car, carrying his walkie-talkie, and set out in pursuit. Timothy Evans came to an eight-foot fence topped by strands of barbed wire. Without hesitation, he soared over it, leaving several fragments of his clothing and his epidermis on the wire. The pursuing officer reported this on his radio, found a less hazardous route, and continued the pursuit.

Several blocks away, a foot patrolman still on duty picked up the radio signals from the pursuing officer. It was evident that the fugitive was coming his way, so he stepped into the shadows of a nearby store entrance. When Timothy Evans came flying past, he gave chase. The quarry by now was somewhat winded, and the officer caught up with him, tackled him, and hung on despite furious resistance. The second officer arrived and finally the two policmen subdued Evans, handcuffed him, and took him to jail. Thus ended the Glorious Fourth for all concerned.

Next day, guess what? Mr. Evans is released on bond. Never mind two actual rapes and an attempted third one. Never mind leaving the scene of a crime, fleeing from the police, and resisting arrest. He's out on bond. He's back on the street.

Furious, I call the judge and complain. I'm reminded that setting bond is designed to ensure the accused's appearance in court. It has nothing to do with his guilt or innocence, with his known past behavior or his probable future behavior. When a tough-minded chief of police tangles with a liberal-minded judge, the outcome is predictable. The police chief seldom wins.

And to Timothy Evans, the law seems to have no teeth in it, so why should he attempt to mend his ways? About a month later a black woman is coming home at night from a church meeting. Not the most original of thinkers or planners, Timothy Evans is hiding in the bushes along her route. As she comes past, he leaps out, seizes her from behind, hits her in the face several times, then starts dragging her toward an abandoned house not far away.

Again the screams of the victim are heard, this time by an elderly black man who dials 911 and reports the crime. The dispatcher is a good dispatcher; she keeps him on the line so that he is able to give almost a blow-by-blow account of what is going on: the screams of the terrified victim, the sounds of the struggle with the rapist. Almost in a matter of seconds, the cops are there. Again Timothy Evans takes to his heels. Again there is a furious foot chase. Again Evans winds up in jail.

This time he is convicted and sentenced to five years in prison. But is this the end of the story? Not quite. A year and a half later, I get a letter from the director of security in our public schools. He has heard that Timothy Evans, who had also been in various sorts of trouble with the school system, is coming up before the parole board and may be granted a form of parole known as "work release," which could mean that he will be back on the streets again shortly. Am I aware of this?

No, I am not aware, although you'd think the parole board would consider me a logical person to be informed. I have no interest whatsoever in having other citizens attacked or raped, or in having the time of my men devoted to chasing Timothy Evans through endless backyards. I send word that I am coming to appear at the hearing. Then I get in my car and drive all the way to Columbia, a distance of 110 miles.

When I get there, I am told that the parole board has already decided that Timothy Evans has served insufficient time to be considered for parole. Therefore, for the present, he will remain behind bars. I don't know whether word that the Charleston Chief of Police was coming to protest had any part in this decision. In any case, a habitual rapist is kept out of circulation for a little while longer.

But it's getting harder and harder to keep them behind bars. When I first came to Charleston, the law said a prisoner had to serve at least one-third of his sentence before he became eligible for parole. Then that became one-quarter of the sentence. Now they are talking about reducing it to one-fifth.

What's the reason? Lack of prison space.

What's the answer? More prisons, more jails.

Does that cost money? Yes, it does. But unless the American people and their elected representatives start finding the money and finding it fast, they are going to keep right on living in a nightmare in which fear and terror will still rule our streets.

Where prisons are concerned, the whole subject of costs is widely misunderstood. One argument that you hear from the rehabilitationists is that it is very expensive to keep criminals in jail; consequently society saves money by getting them out of jail. They bolster this argument with facts and figures based on the cost of land, bricks, mortar, food, utilities, guards' salaries—all finite and measurable things. Divide the total cost by the number of inmates and you arrive at the cost of maintaining—or detaining—a single prisoner for a year. The cost will vary depending on the facility—ten, twenty, thirty thousand dollars. A lot of money, certainly. We'd save that money if the felon were not there, right? Wrong!

For a long time no real survey was made of what would happen if the felon was not behind bars but was out on the street. Then in 1987 the Rand Corporation made a study of one thousand repeat offenders who were serving time for a variety of crimes. These were the ones whose records showed that they could be counted on to resume a life of crime if they were released. The figures showed that when they were at large, these criminals had committed an average of *187 felonies per year*, or a little more than three per week.

The study then tried to compute the cost of such felonies to society. No account was taken for such intangibles as the victims' pain, suffering, or fear. The focus was on monetary loss through the theft of cars or TV sets or silverware, plus the cost of repairing broken windows, kicked-in doors, or other physical damage caused by the felons. Then, to make sure no exaggeration was involved, the study arbitrarily reduced these costs by half. Even so, it was found that the losses caused by these criminals on the loose were *three times* the cost of keeping them behind bars. By releasing such men, usually long before their actual sentences had been served, society was paying a far greater cost, only now that cost was shifted from the taxpayers to the unfortunate victims of the robbers.

This argument probably will not sway the vast army of psychologists, counselors, social workers, and assorted rehabilitationists whose livelihoods depend on perpetuation of the myth that their approach to the crime problem is valid, that leopards do change their spots, that there is a hidden core of goodness in every hardened criminal. They will point with pride to two or three cases out of a hundred where the felon has not repeated his mistakes (which might have happened with no rehabilitation at all) and cling to the notion that somehow their methods can be refined to the point where they can truly deal with the staggering complexities of human personality and motivation and behavior. But in fact they cannot.

When it does happen, rehabilitation comes from inside the former criminal himself. The change takes place in his head. He decides not to be a crook any more, just as he once decided to be one. No one can say exactly what triggers this change; all we can say is that it happens around the age of thirty-five. At that point the number of felons rearrested and sentenced to additional prison terms drops almost to zero.

The change is astounding, really. These men who scorned working take jobs that once they would have spurned. They become taxpayers. They begin to raise families. Sometimes—supreme irony—they become the victims of crime themselves. But it's not the efforts of the rehabilitation industry that causes this. If that were the case, they would have been rehabilitated on their first or second or third incarceration. It has something to do with their biological clock, something that our penal system needs to study and understand better than it does now.

The concept of rehabilitation is a beguiling one. Everyone likes to restore a falling-down house, tune up a wheezy old car, tinker with a balky outboard motor. Religion tells us that there's always hope for the worst sinner, maybe even Jack the Ripper or the Boston Strangler.

But reality is something else. Insurance companies will insure a pianist's hands or a quarterback's knees, but they won't insure the behavior of a released felon or indemnify anyone harmed by one. They're too smart to take the risk. The parole board member may recommend that a convicted rapist be freed, but he won't welcome him with open arms if he moves next door. Human beings are too complex. Human behavior is too unpredictable. Rehabilitation is a noble dream, perhaps, but it is also mostly wishful thinking. Liberals may disagree, but as someone said, a liberal is just a conservative who hasn't been mugged yet.

I'm afraid there's more than a grain of truth in that axiom.

17
How to Make Sure That a Murderer Has Killed His Last Victim

I believe in the death penalty. It is the only way we can be certain that a vicious murderer has killed his last victim. It is the only way that society can proclaim unmistakably that the unlawful taker of an innocent life forfeits his own right to live.

The only criminal act from which the victim cannot possibly recover is homicide. It seems to me that it then follows, both logically and morally, that the killer should share his victim's fate. This is not revenge on the part of society. It is an act of requital where one who takes the greatest of all gifts from a fellow human being thereby loses it for himself.

We emphasize the value of human life when we impose the death penalty on those who kill others. That word "kill" is central to any debate on the death penalty. Everyone—and I mean absolutely *everyone*—of the 2,050 people presently on death row has been convicted of killing a fellow human being. Not only has each one killed someone, but most have been convicted of killing someone while engaged in some other crime, such as burglary, armed robbery, sexual assault, or similar serious offense. There is no one on death row who merely got into a pool hall argument that resulted in a fight where someone was killed. There is no one on death row who merely became involved in a domestic dispute and in a rage reached for some weapon and blindly struck out at another family member and killed him.

Nor is anyone on death row today for having committed the crime of rape alone, or any other kind of sexual assault alone. Today it is the *murder* of his victim that lands the criminal on death row. In the past, much of the opposition to the death penalty centered around its being applied to the crime of rape. Dreadful though that crime is, the victim does survive. To many, the crime did not deserve the death penalty. To some it did, especially when the rapist was black and the victim white, thereby triggering the ancient racial-sexual taboos and passions we're all familiar with.

With rape alone removed as an offense deserving of death, the arguments for and against the death penalty have become clearer and sharper. The Supreme Court has ruled both directly and indirectly that the imposition of the death penalty is not unconstitutional per se. This, of course, leaves the argument essentially unresolved.

One side claims that the death penalty can act as a deterrent, causing potential killers to stop and "think twice" before they kill anyone. The other side cites statistics purporting to show that this is not so. This argument is blurred, at least in the case of our own judicial system, by the *delay* factor. To have any real deterrent effect, the death penalty would have to be carried out promptly enough so that the potential murderer would see it as a key factor in his personal decision to kill or not to kill. Such is not the situation in our country today.

The chief prosecutor of a large judicial circuit recently stated that, even assuming a killer was apprehended within minutes of his commission of a homicide and was tried and convicted within a few weeks, it would be impossible in most states to carry out the death penalty against him in less than eight years. Even if the killer confessed and pleaded guilty, thereby removing the need for a lengthy trial, that would have little effect on the slow pace toward the enactment of the death penalty. In one way, such delays serve a useful purpose in that they give plenty of time for proof of innocence, if any exists, to emerge. Thus the chances that somehow an innocent person may be executed are reduced to a minimum.

Opponents of the death penalty claim that a life sentence is just as effective when it comes to preventing a killer from killing again. But this is not true. Unless the sentence specifically provides that there be no parole, a life sentence killer may indeed be released— and may indeed kill again, as has often been the case.

Ours is a country that values life. But why should we value the lives of killers more than we value the lives of their innocent victims? If the opponents of capital punishment in this country ultimately have their way, many innocent people will die and hundreds of the guilty will continue to live—and sometimes kill again. It is precisely to prevent such injustice that the death penalty deserves to be retained—and resolutely carried out.

18
Black-on-Black Crime: A National Tragedy

Americans believe they have the right to live in a safe community where people respect property and place high value on human life. But most urban blacks don't live in such communities. While it may sound good to say that everyone values human life, the facts suggest otherwise. Recent FBI figures show that in forty-five percent of all homicides the victims are black, and nearly all the perpetrators of these homicides are black also. That means blacks are killing blacks at a rate four times greater than their percentage of the national population. This is a tragic and terrifying fact.

Let me move closer to home. During my first five years of service in Charleston, there were fifty-nine homicides, all but one resulting in an arrest, all but two ending in a conviction. Three whites were killed by three other whites. Two whites were killed by blacks. And fifty-four blacks were killed by fifty-four other blacks. All but two of the killings were the direct result of arguments or disputes between people who knew each other.

We blacks kill one another at a rate that is almost unbelievable, close to ten thousand a year. Your chances of being murdered are highest if you are a black male between the ages of fifteen and twenty-four. The statistics also show that most likely your murderer will be someone who lives within two hundred yards of your home.

Blacks often kill one another for the most trivial of reasons. When blacks kill whites it is most often for money. But when they kill other blacks it can be for any reason, or sometimes no reason at all.

Not many members of the black community seem to get upset about this. We act as if this state of affairs is inevitable, almost normal. But let a white person kill a black for whatever reason, even self-defense, and there is an immediate outcry from the black community. If the white person is a police officer, the protests are quadrupled. There are marches, speeches, and threats, while often in the same week one black will kill another over a five-dollar gambling debt and not a peep is heard. Even black newspapers seldom bother to report such incidents.

We blacks are not going to be able to convince many people that we consider black lives to be valuable if we react with indifference when our own people cut, beat, stab, and shoot one another. Where are the speech-makers and protesters when one black plunges a knife into the heart of another as a way of settling—permanently—an argument over who knows what? I can tell you, they're hard to find.

The problem of the black crime rate in urban centers is basically ours. The federal government can't solve it for us. White people can't solve it for us. No one can

resolve the tragedy of black-on-black crime but ourselves.

Can we do it? I think so. But we're going to have to
ask ourselves some tough questions. And we are going
to have to change some attitudes.

When I first came to Charleston as police chief, the
police weren't considered the friends and protectors of
black citizens. They were more like an army of occupation, feared and resented, suspected of harboring racist
feelings, sometimes accused of outright brutality.

As for the black attitude toward crime in general, it
was a fact of life. Sure, there were domestic quarrels
where people—black people—were beaten or shot or
stabbed, usually by other black people. Sure, there were
fights in bars that quite often ended in homicide. Sure,
the streets were full of teenagers who had no jobs and
no money and whose chosen solution to this sorry state
of affairs was to go out looking for someone to rob. So
what? The police were supposed to take action against
such things, but it never occurred to most black people
to try to help the police. Who wants to be a snitch?
Who wants to get involved? Nobody.

Resentment of cops. Passive acceptance of crime. A
pall of inertia and indifference hung over the whole
city. You could feel it. You could almost smell it.

Until one night a sudden tragedy changed everything.

It was about nine-thirty on a late summer evening.
The Reverend William Capers, respected black pastor
of the Mount Pisgah Baptist Church, was standing outside the little brick building with five elderly members
of his church board, who had just concluded a meeting.
The Reverend Capers, in his forties, was the youngest
of the group.

Suddenly there appeared three black teenagers, aged
thirteen, fourteen, and fifteen. They didn't know the

Reverend Capers or any of his friends. They were simply looking for someone to rob. They walked up to the Reverend Capers and asked him for a dollar.

When the minister refused, one of the assailants pulled out a .22-caliber pistol. Shouting obscenities, he ordered the minister to give him all his money. The Reverend Capers told the gang angrily that he had none and that what they were doing was wrong. Perhaps he might have been less forthright if he had known that, only a few months earlier, the two older boys had approached a man in a telephone booth, asked for a quarter, and when he refused, shot him dead. They had been sent to a juvenile correctional facility but were soon released.

The Reverend's words of condemnation infuriated them. "Shoot him!" the oldest boy said to his companion with the gun. When the command was not instantly obeyed, he shouted, "Give me the gun! I'll do it!" Shamed into it, the kid with the gun pulled the trigger. The minister fell with a bullet in his spine. The assailants took his money, beat and robbed the terrified elderly board members, and melted into the shadows. The whole episode took less than ninety seconds.

If an ordinary pedestrian had been shot in the course of a mugging, that would have been considered by the black community and others as just another street crime. I knew instantly that this was no ordinary crime and that it would evoke no ordinary reaction. I knew it would infuriate the entire community.

A *minister* had been shot. Standing in front of his own *church* he had been gunned down in cold blood. He would be paralyzed for life. This was beyond the pale. This was more than people could or would stand. I knew the wall of black indifference to crime would be breached, at least in this case. I knew the reluctance of blacks to help the police would be overcome. If we could just grasp the opportunity this tragedy offered, black disinterest in crime reduction might become a thing of the past.

Fortunately, the case had no racial angle at all. The assailants were black, the victims were black, no police— white or black—had been involved. I did all I could to amplify public reaction. I said it was the most dastardly crime that had occurred since my arrival in Charleston. I said we needed help in solving it, especially help from the black community. And we got it. Scores of tips poured in. Within twenty-four hours we had eyewitness accounts of the shooting. Our star witness was a twelve-year-old black kid who was on his way to the grocery store. He heard the shot and saw the minister fall. The assailants knew the kid had seen them. They even offered to share the stolen money with him if he agreed to say nothing. But he went home and told his parents.

His father reacted in the traditional fashion. It's not our business. Let's stay out of it. But the kid's mother ignored her husband. She brought the youngster down to the police station to tell us his story.

Seeing the crime happen was one thing; identifying the criminal was another. I assigned one of our black female detectives, Hazel Giles, to the case. I also assigned Joe Lalima, a white male detective. That same night, working with sources she had in the black community, Hazel learned that an agitated black woman had been going about a certain neighborhood trying to borrow money "for a bus ticket to New York." She did in fact raise the money. She even sold the pistol used in the crime to send her son to the boy's father in New York. Misplaced loyalty, certainly, but the maternal instinct is a very strong force.

Now that the kid was a fugitive in another state, we called the FBI. By checking the woman's telephone bill and the number she had been calling in New York, the

FBI was able to pinpoint the address where the kid was hiding, arrest the boy, and send him back to us. He expressed surprise, having previously killed one man, at all the commotion about a wounded minister. "Man, he ain't even *dead*, is he?"

We picked up the other two kids. The youngest turned state's evidence; the older two went to prison. Not a very stiff sentence. At least, the Reverend Capers didn't think it was adequate. And neither did I. But out of evil had come this good: the climate had changed. All the prayer meetings. All the editorials in the newspapers. All the rewards offered—the twelve-year-old witness did share in that. All the tips from informers. These things had galvanized the black community, which was now conditioned to help cops, not fear or ignore them. Where the black community once had focused almost entirely on the issue of police brutality, now it was willing to give information and help solve crimes.

It was a sensational turnaround in attitude. And it persists in Charleston to this day.

Unfortunately, that turnaround hasn't happened in many cities across the land. The situation in the slum areas remains grim. In the most disadvantaged segment of the black population—somewhere between five and seven million people—one out of every two persons lives in poverty, one family out of two has no father, one out of two teenagers has no job, one out of four births is to a teenager and most of these are illegitimate.

It's a bleak and hopeless society of women without husbands and men without work. Cocaine-related deaths for blacks tripled in a recent two-year period. Out of every thousand new jobs created in the last decade, young black men were able to land only one. When more fortunate blacks move up the social or pro-

fessional ladder and escape from the ghetto, they leave
behind a vacuum in which the chief role models for
youngsters are the street crime specialists or the drug
pushers with their fancy clothes and flashy automobiles.
Meanwhile, as industries move from the central city to
the suburbs, jobs go with them, out of reach of poor
blacks who lack transportation and can't afford to ride
the bus—assuming there is a bus.

It's a grim picture, all right, if you look only at the
big cities. Fortunately, there is a bright spot: the rural
areas, where we find the lowest incidence of black crime,
especially black-on-black crime. Why should this be so
in rural areas, where poverty is greatest, education
weakest, political participation lowest, and unemploy-
ment highest?

The answer has to lie in the realm of values. Family
cohesion and marital relationships are stronger in rural
areas. The influence of the church is stronger there.
And our rural brethren have even more going for them
than that. Among rural folk of all backgrounds, people
are still held accountable for what they do. You don't
hear rural blacks making excuses for black criminals or
street thugs who won't work even when work is available. Black kids who grow up in small towns or in the
country are more likely to have both parents on hand
to teach basic values and enforce them. "Don't let me
catch you stealing! Don't tell lies! Don't you dare drop
out of school; I'll skin you alive if you do!"

You're *accountable*, you're *responsible* for what you do.
That's the key message, hammered home day after day.
If you go off the track, don't blame poverty. Don't
blame racism. Don't blame lack of opportunity. Blame
yourself.

If we are going to revitalize our urban culture, we
are going to have to do it with the values that worked
for us in the past and still work in some parts of this

country: respect for property, respect for law, respect for each other, respect for human life. Community cooperation. Hard work, and no excuses. Ostracism for those who refuse to play by the rules. Somehow we have to dust off and rediscover the same ideas and the same values that were emphasized so steadily and so effectively by schools and churches and parents fifty or seventy-five years ago. In those days, a thief was no hero. In those days, a drug user was a freak—a dope fiend. In those days women hadn't traded their husbands for welfare checks. In those days babies of unwed mothers weren't growing up to have illegitimate babies of their own.

If the restoration of values was given top educational priority in a national program that had all the urgency of the crash program that put men on the moon, would such a program work? Perhaps it might if the system, using the latest and best educational techniques, could develop people like Marva Collins, the remarkable black schoolteacher in Chicago who got such sensational results with black children who had been written off as almost hopeless. "You're black," she would tell them. "Be proud of it! You've got a first-class mind. Use it! You can do anything you make up your mind to do. You can be anything, succeed at anything. Don't ever think failure. You're not going to fail because I won't let you fail!"

Marva Collins had those kids so fired up that they were reading Dickens and Shakespeare in sixth grade and successfully tackling high school math and loving it. Meanwhile, they were being programmed not to lie, not to steal, not to cheat, not to mess with drugs. They were sold on the idea that these are things that strong, bright, successful, worthwhile people just do not do. Stealing is *wrong*. Therefore if you steal, *you* are wrong.

Who wants to be wrong when it puts you at a disadvantage in life?

The most powerful motivating force in the world is self-interest. Under a teacher like Marva Collins, kids can grasp the astonishing idea that good behavior is a plus, something that will pay off for them. This is the attitude that needs so desperately to be reborn in the slums and ghettos, the breeding places of crime.

Other attitudes need changing too. We blacks need to overcome our fear and distrust of the police and be the first to volunteer information on those among us who steal and rob, sell dope to our children, engage in prostitution, commit murder, resist arrest. We have to work together to destroy the small but potent criminal subculture that is thriving in so many of our communities. We have to be willing to enter all phases of the criminal justice system. We need more black judges, lawyers, DAs. We especially need more blacks in uniform, because that is where the action is and where the key decisions are made. More discretionary authority (and perhaps more justice) is exercised by a uniformed police officer than by any other participant in the criminal justice process.

Above all, we blacks should know by now that if our lives, our communities, our values, and our standards are going to change for the better, that change is not going to come from the government or from other racial groups. It must come from us.

The only helping hand we are ever likely to see is right there on the end of our arm. We have to find the leadership, we have to find the brains and determination and pride inside our own community, inside our own race.

And now, if I may, I'd like to pay a brief tribute to the man who saw that vision, who held fast to that dream, even though it cost him his life.

19
Requiem For a Fallen Leader

Assassins have destroyed great Americans through the years, all the way from Abraham Lincoln to John F. Kennedy and Martin Luther King.

Dr. Martin Luther King should be at the head of every list of black heroes. I know he's at the head of mine. The greatest loss to black Americans was the death of Dr. King. There is no black citizen in this country who doesn't owe a tremendous debt to the quiet pastor who had a dream of a better world for all people, black and white. But for him, probably no black mayor would hold office, as they now do in many great cities. But for him, I would never even have been considered for the job I now hold as police chief of Charleston, South Carolina.

There are many other heroes to whom black Americans owe much. Rosa Parks and her quiet struggle for dignity that led to the Montgomery bus boycott, the leadership of men like A. Phillip Randolph and Thurgood Marshall. The courage of Jackie Robinson. The sacrifice of the slain civil rights workers: Andrew Goodman, James Chaney, Michael Schwerner, Medgar Evers. The patience and persistence of all the marchers and picketers and boycotters of the 1960s.

But in the eyes of history, Martin Luther King towers above them all. The list of progressive things that Dr. King brought about, with the help of others, is almost endless. To name a few:

Voting rights for black Americans.

Election of blacks to public office.

Reduction of police brutality.

Increased black participation in business enterprises.

Opportunities for quality education.

Better housing for all low-income people.

Equal access to public accommodations.

I never met Dr. King, but I did see him once. It was in 1965. I was in the San Francisco International Airport, waiting to catch a plane, when I heard the announcer say on the public address system: "Dr. Martin Luther King, Dr. Martin Luther King, please pick up the white courtesy telephone." That alerted everyone in the airport to the fact that he was right there among us. I remember thinking at the time how fitting it was that a man who had dedicated his life to ending segregation in buses, rest rooms, lunch counters, and airports was summoned to a "white" phone; the reference to the color no longer had a double meaning, thanks to this very man.

Martin Luther King's enemies used to call him a radical. Some still do. But he was no radical. He was a moderate who often used his influence to restrain radicals. After Rosa Parks was arrested in Montgomery in 1955 for refusing to give up her seat in the white section of a bus to permit a white man to sit down, there was much agitation among black people, and much anger, and even a bit of rabble-rousing. A group of people gathered who were determined to push for an immediate end to segregated seating on the city's buses, even if it meant resorting to violence. Dr. King defused this time bomb and calmed the agitators. It is my belief that segregation ended sooner in America than it would have if the rabble-rousers had been encouraged rather than restrained by Dr. King.

It seems incredible to me, when one looks back and sees how far we have come, that there are black people today who go around saying that things are worse now than ever before. I don't see how they can possibly say that. The truth is there has never been a time in the history of this country when life was better for any American, black or white.

We have more blacks holding positions of responsibility in government, politics, education, and business than ever before. I wouldn't have believed it if anyone had told me in 1962, the year I graduated from high school in Houston, that in a single generation the police chiefs of Houston, New York City, Detroit, Baltimore, Chicago, Atlanta, Miami, New Orleans, and even Charleston would be black.

In 1963 when Governor George Wallace of Alabama stood at the schoolhouse door to block the admission of black children, who would have thought that his attitude would change so completely that the day would come when the very same man would be awarded and proudly display an Honorary Doctorate of Humanities from the famous black Tuskegee University?

Who would have believed that for every black enrolled in college in 1960 there would be eight in 1980?

When Jackie Robinson hit his first home run for a major league team in 1947, who could have foreseen the dominance of blacks in organized sports today?

To pretend for political, social, academic, or any other reason that things are worse than ever is an insult to the memories of Dr. Martin Luther King, Jr., the slain civil rights workers, and the poor little girls who were blinded or killed in the Birmingham church bombing. We black people in this country have known far worse times than these. As I visit the beautiful plantations and gardens of historical Charleston, the antebellum mansions of Mobile and Montgomery, I often think of the pain and suffering of old tired black women trudging along those same lanes which were then mere footpaths, hauling a load of wash to the Big House. I wonder if they would have thought that life for us today is worse than it ever has been for black people. I think not.

This country has come a long way. We have accomplished much. But the struggle for equal opportunity and human dignity is not over. The battle for full participation in American society has not yet been fully won. That struggle must continue, as Dr. King would have wished it to.

I remember vividly the day Dr. King was awarded the Nobel Peace Prize in 1964. I was a student at San Francisco State College then. A Lutheran minister, a friend of mine, came running up to me with the news. I can remember him saying joyously that "we" got the Nobel Peace Prize. And it *was* "we." It was all of us who worked in the civil rights movement in San Francisco, in Atlanta, and in Montgomery, all who toiled along the dusty red clay roads of Mississippi, or pounded the picket lines in San Francisco and elsewhere. It was an important recognition by the world that a monumental and long-delayed change in human relationships was at last underway.

Dr. King was felled by an assassin's bullet on April

4, 1968. The killer shot Dr. King in an attempt to silence him and thus eliminate his influence. Ironically, when he killed the man, he magnified his ideas and his memory and perpetuated his influence far beyond any natural life span Dr. King might have had.

In the year 1776, a bold experiment was begun in this country. An experiment in democracy and a faith in humanity which asserted that all men are created equal, that all people should have equal access to life's benefits; that there should be opportunity and justice for all. We haven't reached these goals completely, but who can deny that much progress has been made? The words said to have been uttered by an old black woman who had spent most of a lifetime in slavery sum it up best:

> We ain't what we want to be;
> We ain't what we oughta be;
> We ain't what we're goin' to be;
> But, thank God, we ain't what we wuz.

And now, perhaps, it's time for me to take a backward glance and trace the path that led me from a poor section of segregated Houston to the challenging job I hold in Charleston today.

20
Black—Before It Became Beautiful

The earliest recollection I have of anything was the death of my older brother. He was about five. I must have been three or four. To this day, I'm not sure what caused his death; I just remember him in some sort of paroxysm or convulsion on the bathroom floor in our little two-bedroom house in Houston. I'm told that I went around calling for him for quite a long time after he died, which upset everyone, especially my mother, who naturally was upset enough by the death of her firstborn. She went on to have five more children after me—all in a span of nine years—but I think she never got over losing her first one.

I have very dark skin, like my mother. Some of my brothers and sisters are much lighter. My father is very light-skinned. His father was a Russian Jew named Sol Greenberg, who came from the Ukraine to America and somehow found his way to Texas. There in that rough Western country at the turn of the century he met and fell in love with a black woman. They had two children, both of them light-skinned. Marriage between a white man and a black woman would have been unthinkable, illegal in fact, in Texas in those days.

The family name was shortened to Green, and that, of course, was the name our family used when we were growing up in Houston. The Jewishness of his white father, who died before I was born, meant nothing to him, and so it meant nothing to us kids either. We children were brought up as Methodists, my mother's religion. I did not start using my grandfather's last name, Greenberg, until I was in college, when my identification with Jewish values first began.

My father's relatives didn't associate with the rest of us much because they were trying to distance themselves from the blackness in the family. "Black is beautiful" was a concept that hadn't been born yet. In fact, blackness was considered a badge of inferiority. In those days "black" didn't mean Negro, as it does today, it meant black in skin color. Sometimes, when they got angry with me, my light-skinned brothers and sisters would call me "you old black so-and-so." This insult implied that they thought they were superior because the color of their skin was lighter—superior to my brother Donald and me and, of course, better than my mother, because she too was dark.

There were six of us kids in our little house. I was born in 1943. After me came Donald, the other dark-skinned one, and a bit of a loner. He was killed in Vietnam. Next came Herbert, who was very bright. He's still in Houston, working for the government. After Herbert came my sister Carolyn, clearly our father's pet. I used to wonder why he preferred her to all the rest of us. She was never punished for anything, or hardly ever.

After Carolyn came Bertram, a bit of a rascal, always

in trouble when we were growing up. You might say he was—and is—the white sheep of the family. Then came my youngest sister Sharon, probably the smartest of us. She works for a large corporation in Houston.

I can never remember a time in Houston when my father was unemployed or when my mother was out of a job. Our dad was an agent for a black-owned insurance company that sold policies to black people. That meant he wore a coat and tie and worked with a pen or pencil, not with his hands. My mother worked as a maid for various white families in Houston. She had great respect for manual labor; as a child she had picked cotton in the fields, and that was *work*, as she understood it.

I think the sort of job my father had struck my mother as a kind of evasion of real work. But he was happy with it because, for one thing, in a black company he was not at the mercy of white bosses. He was like a black preacher in that respect—no white person could fire him. At one point, during World War II, he had been a machinist in a shipyard. Then, after he was laid off, he had shined shoes in a barbershop where all the customers were white. He probably made as much money from tips as he later earned with the insurance company. But in the barbershop he had to listen to the ethnic jokes and racial slurs that the patrons bandied about. I've always been amazed at how some white people can disregard the presence of black people, tune them out altogether, treat them as if they were furniture or some other inanimate object. I think my father's aversion to white people stemmed partly from that.

The way we had to live says something about the wages paid in those days. Even with two sources of income, we were a poor family in a very poor neighborhood. Two adults and six children crowded into a two-bedroom frame house on McGowan Street that was just like all the other shabby houses on the street. No doubt if you were a slumlord and owned enough ramshackle houses you could get rich. At least, you could if you kept repairs and maintenance to an absolute minimum, which is what most slumlords did. Our landlord, I remember, was an Italian. My father had no use for white people in general, but he disliked Italians especially, and I think his prejudice came from years and years of paying rent to this man and feeling exploited and helpless to do anything about it.

I never was close to my father, who still lives in Houston. I'm not close to him today—in fact, we have little contact with each other. But I remember him well in the years of my childhood because he was such a strong personality. You might not love him. You might not even like him. But you couldn't ignore him.

He had a rigid set of beliefs. He believed that in any activity or project there was one right way. You had to figure out the right way, and in our family that simply meant doing things *his* way. There was no room for discussion or disagreement or experimentation. It had to be his way or not at all.

I never heard my father offer a word of praise or encouragement to any of us children, with the possible exception of Carolyn. His preferred form of discipline with the boys was whacking us on the palm of the hand with a leather belt. No doubt we deserved it sometimes, but it hurt a lot and I often went around with a swollen hand. The last time I can remember being whacked was when I was about fourteen. I went into the girls' bedroom one day to look for something and found Carolyn only half-dressed. She snatched up some clothes, held them in front of her, and began screaming, "Stop looking at me, stop looking at me!" She was clutching a blouse to her chest. I said, "What's the big

deal? Just a couple of raisins on a pair of pancakes!"
Of course, that made her even madder. She told our
father, and I really got whacked.

As far as I was concerned, the less we saw of our
father the better. I disliked Sundays and holidays, because then he'd be at home. I think my main resentment
of him stemmed from the way he treated our mother.
If he ever showed her any warmth or tenderness or
kindness, I never saw it. She was a fighter, though, and
would stand up to him when she had to. Like many
black women, she got consolation and companionship
from her religion.

I don't know what made our father the way he was.
His attitude toward us was basically very simple: he
believed a kid deserved to be fed. That was it. Nothing
more. If you needed new shoelaces, too bad. Pocket
money? Forget it! If you want it, earn it.

We went to a neighborhood school that was completely segregated. All black. This was in the early
1950s, before the 1954 Supreme Court decision deseg-
regating the schools. My brother Donald and I failed
first grade, I remember. Not because we were dumb,
but because we had to take turns staying home to look
after the smaller children while our mother was at work.
No day-care centers in those days. No money for baby-
sitters. One week I'd go to school Monday, Wednesday
and Friday, while Donald (who was only about six himself) stayed home. Next week, he'd go to school for
three days and I'd stay home. Naturally, missing half
our classes, we had a tough time that first year. Later
on, when the younger children were old enough to look
after themselves, Donald and I caught up easily enough.

One good thing about this odd arrangement was that,
when the time came for the younger kids to go to school,
they already knew how to read because Donald and I

taught them. Doing our homework on the days we had
to stay home, we simply showed the younger kids how
to read. So when they finally went to school, they were
well ahead of the game. I guess we had our own private
Head Start program.

When I was a kid going to that segregated black
school in Houston, I always liked that phrase in the
Pledge of Allegiance, "liberty and justice for all." As a
black I recognized, of course, that it didn't really apply
to me. But I understood that it referred to the high
principles this country was founded on, and I felt good
about that. Obviously, a lot of those principles weren't
operative in my case, but on the other hand a lot of
them were. And I was convinced at that age—as I'm
convinced today—that blacks in the United States, bad
though our situations may be sometimes, are nonetheless better off, materially and socially, than we would
be in almost any other country.

I believed that when I was a kid, and I believe it now.
I wouldn't leave this country and go somewhere else
to live, and I think that is true of most blacks. If this
were not the case, more blacks would have drifted toward the Communist Party or would have expatriated
themselves. To emigrate to Europe or to Africa may
have seemed like a solution for some black intellectuals
in the past. But most chose to remain here. I think
they were right.

Our school may have had its limitations, but I enjoyed
it. Most of the time we had no spending money, but a
lot of kids in the neighborhood had the same problem.
I used to earn a dollar or two by going to work with
my mother and running errands or cutting grass—anything the family she worked for wanted done. Some of
these families were Jewish. It may seem odd to anyone
who is neither black nor Jewish, but in those days our
family and a lot of other black families regarded Jews

as being less hostile to blacks than other whites were. We didn't think of them as angels (after all, they were still white), but we felt they were less likely to cause us trouble than non-Jewish Caucasians. We trusted them a bit more, perhaps because we knew they were discriminated against themselves.

I remember a remark my father once made that reflected this attitude. One day, in the mid-fifties when the Montgomery bus boycott was on in Alabama and racial feelings were running high, my sister Carolyn had gone into downtown Houston. She was wearing a pair of those open-toed sandals called thongs, or flip-flops, and a white man accidentally stepped on her foot, hard enough to make it bleed. By the time she got home, her foot was quite swollen. She showed it to my father and, knowing the animosity he had for most white people, she told him what she thought he wanted to hear. She didn't say, "Somebody stepped on my foot," or "A man stepped on my foot by accident." She said, "A *white* man stepped on my foot."

That was all it took to enrage my father. "That white son of a bitch," he shouted. "Stepping on my daughter's foot!" (Don't forget, Carolyn was his pet.)

Then he saw that a handkerchief was wrapped around my sister's big toe. "Where'd you get that handkerchief?" he asked. By now it was dirty from dragging in the street, but it was obviously an expensive linen one.

Carolyn said, "Oh, the man took it out of his pocket. He looked at my toe. Then he tied it up with his handkerchief."

The thought of a white man in downtown Houston caring enough to bend down and tie up a black girl's foot to provide some relief, some cleanliness, blew my father's mind. He was silent for a moment. Then he said, "Oh! Probably one of the Jews down there." And all the anger and indignation seemed to drain out of him.

With reactions and comments like that in our house, it was easy to get the notion that, somehow, Jews weren't as bad or as hostile as other whites, that even if you were black you had a fairly good chance of communicating or interacting with them. And this belief was reinforced by my mother, who at various times worked for Jewish families.

I remember puzzling, as a youngster, over the anti-Semitism that existed in Houston. I thought that whites didn't like us blacks because we were black. We had different characteristics: thick lips, kinky hair. I figured that was the reason why blacks—even highly educated blacks—had to sit in the back of the bus and couldn't go to "white" movies.

But I couldn't understand why Christian whites would dislike Jewish whites. How could they even tell that a person was Jewish? For the most part, Jews look like other whites. Some are blue-eyed. Some are blond. Some are tall, some are short. It seemed to me that you knew a person was Jewish only because someone told you he was Jewish or because he had an obviously Jewish name.

Jews did feel discrimination, but not to the same extent. They could sit in the front of the bus; they went to any restaurant they wanted and sat where they chose to sit; they could try on clothes in department stores. Blacks couldn't do any of those things. Yet Jews couldn't belong to the country club. And some people wouldn't vote for them if they tried to run for public office.

People who disliked Jews handed their prejudices down to their children. They said that Jews loved money and that all of them were rich. I knew that wasn't true because I saw too many poor Jews. The Jews my mother

worked for had more than we did. They were never
hungry or afraid of being put out on the street, as we
sometimes were. But when I'd go to their houses to do
odd jobs, I'd hear them worrying about finances,
struggling to pay their bills. To say that these people
were rich was ridiculous.

There was no question about it in my mind—Jews
treated blacks differently from the way other whites
treated blacks. The automatic hostility, the built-in con-
descension just weren't there. Oh, sometimes I would
hear anti-Semitic remarks from blacks. As a black, you
hear remarks that are essentially racist where all whites
are concerned. But by and large, in those days, blacks
weren't as anti-Semitic as most whites. One thing in my
experience has been true all along, and I haven't found
a single exception to it: if you find a person who is
anti-Semitic, that person is anti-black. It works the other
way, too: if a person is anti-black, he is also anti-Semitic.
It's almost as if that sort of prejudice is all encompas-
sing.

There were no Jews in our school, of course; it was
all black. We never had any school buses. We walked
to school or took the public bus. A school kid with a
pass could ride the public bus for a nickel. No nickel
meant no ride. I had to walk.

I never had the fancy clothes that some of the kids
in our school had. These were middle-class black kids,
which meant they were the sons or daughters of black
ministers, school teachers, doctors, dentists, perhaps a
lawyer or two. The clothes barrier made it difficult for
us poorer kids to be invited to join the social clubs that
the Jack & Jills or Beau Brummels, as we called them,
belonged to. I was excluded not only because I didn't
dress as they did, but kids with skin as dark as mine
also didn't fit into the lighter-skinned group. And I

resented this exclusion because academically I could easily equal or outperform them. I was usually among the top ten, though never first or second.

I remember one day a girl I was going with, who belonged to one of the middle-class groups, invited me to a prom. Well, I accepted, but I couldn't come up with a tuxedo, which was required dress for the dance. I just didn't have the money to rent one. "Can't you just wear a dark suit?" she asked. But I didn't have a dark suit either. I had only one suit, and it wasn't dark. I remember the look of amazement on that girl's face. She just couldn't conceive of a boy not having a dark suit.

It's funny how these petty humiliations stick in your mind. She never forgave me for standing her up, as she put it. And I never forgave her for not understanding that I just didn't have the things her other friends had.

Above and beyond these little incidents was an atmosphere of fear that became the constant companion of a young black male growing up in Houston in the fifties and sixties. The civil rights movement was getting underway. I remember blacks being arrested when they attempted to attend services in white churches. They were turned away by the deacons or church officials, and if they persisted the police were called. In fact, in many instances, the police were already at the church because the blacks had announced in advance that the attempt would be made.

The fear we felt didn't come from these church confrontations, although they added to the existing tension. The real fear was that white anger at black attempts to end segregation might turn on us as a target whether we had been directly involved or not.

I remember when I was about fifteen having a job

of sorts in a small hotel out in North Houston. I used to get to work on the bus. At about this time—it must have been around 1959—a black man was alleged to have raped a white woman. Quite possibly he did rape her; in any case, the police were looking for him. That was understandable, but what bothered my mother and me was that other whites were also looking for him. Self-appointed vigilantes, really—and we knew they wouldn't be too concerned about whether they got the right man or not. They were out to get a black, any black, that was for sure.

And that was what really frightened us, because I had to go to work at a hotel in an area not far from where this crime had been committed. I was afraid to go to work. But we needed the money. It was an after-school job, which meant that it was dark when I finished work. And I had to stand on the corner and wait for the bus; there was no other way to get home.

As I waited on the corner, cars would drive by, some-times circle the block and come back so that the occu-pants could look me over again and try to figure out whether I was the rapist they were looking for. I was afraid that even if they weren't convinced I was the right guy, they might be mean enough or angry enough—or maybe drunk enough—to grab me. Some black had to pay.

My sense of panic was heightened by uneasiness about my father's rather outspoken antipathy for racial discrimination. What if his views were known? What if some racist whites were aware that he had been giving support and encouragement to a group of young black college kids who were deeply influenced by the civil rights movement then catching fire in Alabama, Missis-sippi, and Georgia? What if they resented the indepen-dence he had as a black employee of a black insurance company? What if some night when the bus stopped, a gang of rednecks boarded it and dragged me off, to be taken somewhere and mutilated or killed? It would be better to be picked up, even mistakenly, by the police. They might beat the hell out of me, but they wouldn't mutilate or kill me.

I finally decided the only way to get home safely was to ask my white employer, Mr. Ward, to give me a ride. I would then be safe because I would be in the company, and therefore under the authority and protection, of a white man.

So I asked Mr. Ward if he could do this. He looked at me for a long moment, then he said he would. And he did. I was grateful to him then, and I'm grateful to him still. It showed me that not every white man is an enemy.

Nobody was likely to bother me while I was under the protection of Mr. Ward, and not just because he was white. He was also very tough. He looked like a typical redneck: tall, barrel-chested, with a huge pot belly and hands like sledge hammers. Truck drivers used to come to the hotel to sleep, and one of my jobs was to keep a lookout to make sure that the truckers didn't bring women up to their rooms. If they did, I would tell Mr. Ward and he would boot them out. He was mean enough and tough enough to do it, too. One of his eyes had a terrible squint—I was never sure who he was looking at—and he had a scar from a knife wound, or maybe a broken bottle slash, that started on his cheek and ran right up through his eyelid and onto his forehead. "If anyone ever tries to mess with you," he told me, "just let me know." He promised he would "beat the crap out of anyone who did."

One day a trucker tried to smuggle a woman into the hotel. I followed the couple to see which room they went into. I waited outside and listened, but I must have made a noise because suddenly the door was jerked open. There stood the trucker, big as a gorilla and twice as ugly. He made a grab for me. "Come here, you little bastard!" he roared. I ran down the hall to the stairs with the trucker right behind me, cursing and gaining on me as I made for the office. I was scared stiff. Mr. Ward heard all the commotion and stepped out. The trucker froze in his tracks. "That nigger was spying on me," he yelled. "I'll kill him!"

Mr. Ward clenched his fists and said, "You ain't goin' to do nothin'!" The trucker backed away and that was the last I saw of him. I guess he collected his girlfriend and departed.

The atmosphere of fear can have a deeply ingrained effect. I remember one day when my mother, my sister Carolyn, one of my brothers, and I had gone downtown to buy things we kids would need for school. I was about twelve or thirteen. And school authorities required all boys my age to wear a jockstrap for gym. I didn't think this was necessary in my case—those things, like mustaches, were for grown-ups. But the school said we had to have them. So my mother had taken us downtown to buy the jockstraps, and Carolyn had come along.

When we got a jockstrap for my brother and one for me, Carolyn wanted one too. "Why can't I have one?" she cried.

Our mother was too embarrassed to explain to her in front of the white sales clerk why she didn't need one. She just said she couldn't have one. Carolyn went flouncing around the store pretending to be angry. She came to the water fountain and decided to have a drink. She was so busy protesting being deprived of a jockstrap that she didn't notice there were two water fountains, both plainly marked, one for Whites and one for Coloreds. She picked the one reserved for whites to drink from.

You know how little kids drink from a water cooler; they put their mouths right down on the hole where the water comes out. That was what Carolyn was doing, not just drinking from the jet of water but putting her mouth right down on the opening itself. We knew the whites wouldn't like that.

My mother said, in a kind of terrified gasp, "Get her!"

I ran to get her, and I can still remember how scared I was. I grabbed her off the little stool where she was standing and kept running with her in my arms until we were out of the store. Then I waited outside for my mother to come. I was breathing hard, partly from exertion, partly from fright. I really expected a horde of whites to appear and attack us with axe handles. And I remember hoping they wouldn't get my mother, even if they got to us.

But nothing happened. Nothing at all. Nobody came after us. Nobody said anything. To this day, I don't know whether anyone was upset or even realized what had happened. But I'll never forget the terror that gripped me when my mother said "Get her!", because I felt we had broken some terrible taboo and this time "they" would get us for sure.

You might think that growing up in these circumstances would have made us hate Caucasians, but it didn't. No one in our family, except perhaps my father, actually hated white people. There was a certain bitter pride in my father, and one thing he taught us, intentionally or unintentionally, was that Caucasians were no better than we were. Just because we were black and they were white didn't mean that they were smarter than we were; it just meant that they were better off than we were. They had more money. They had more power, more acceptance. But there was no reason for us to feel inferior solely because they were white.

Consequently I never had the sense of inferiority that many blacks grew up with. We were poor, we had a lot of problems to cope with. But I came out of my childhood not feeling inferior to anyone.

I had one white friend in those days, a lady I worked for named Mrs. Mangham. I liked her very much, and at the same time I was afraid of her. I was afraid of her because—well, because she was a single woman. I did yard work for her, and sometimes worked in the house. I was about fourteen or fifteen; she was in her forties. To me she seemed quite old. She had been married but now was divorced.

I was afraid that white racists might come after her for treating me as she did. She would always come and get me in her car. She wouldn't let me sit in the back; I had to sit in front with her. She brought back little presents for me when she went shopping: a shirt, a pair of sneakers. We ate the same food at the same table from the same kind of plates. I could go to the stove and get my own food or go to the refrigerator and take what I wanted. She never said anything about my being too sweaty or dirty to come into the house after I had been working in the yard. She forbade anyone to use the word "nigger" in her house—at least in my presence.

If you were a black person in a situation like that, in which white people were treating you as an equal, you had to think some ulterior motive must be involved. I was really afraid that she might get me in trouble by trying to make some sort of pass at me. And that could only spell disaster for me in a racist community like Houston. That was the fear I had, but it turned out to be unfounded with Mrs. Mangham. She was simply being nice to me.

The world, unfortunately, is not composed of Mrs. Manghams. I never was able to deal with the feeling that some people disliked me simply because I was black. If I had been a no-good SOB, it would have been understandable. But to despise me simply because of the color of my skin, that was too much. I think that's the reason why, even today, I find it difficult, even painful, to look at a movie or a play about racial discrimination. There are many, many whites whom I prefer to a great many blacks—not because they're white, but because of the kind of people they are. But this whole idea of race as the determining factor in social relationships makes no sense at all.

I never suffered any physical violence from whites when I was growing up in the fifties and sixties. I was never roughed up by police. I was never beaten or manhandled by any Caucasian. Perhaps because that was when cracks were beginning to appear in the ancient racial barriers. But the threat was always there. The fear was always there.

I remember walking home from high school one day and seeing a car coming down the street toward me. The car pulled over to the curb and waited for me to pass. There was a white man sitting in it. I remember looking directly into his face. He had steel blue eyes. He said, "Do you know anything about a white woman and a Negro man living together anywhere around here?"

I said that I didn't. If something like that *was* going on in the area I would have known about it. People would have been talking.

He seemed to read my thoughts. He said, "Are you sure you haven't heard any of the old folks talking about a white woman living with a Negro man?"

I said, "No, sir, I haven't heard anybody talking," which was true. I hadn't. He said, "Okay," and let me go. He didn't threaten me in any way. He was a plainclothes detective, or said he was. He drove off, and I walked away, and I never told anybody that this had happened.

Blacks have always known that whites are intensely interested in anything having to do with sex between white women and black men. The old folks in the black community used to tell us that if they called the authorities about a burglary or some such happening the police would take forever to respond. But if you told them a white woman was being chased or raped by a black man, the cops would be on the spot faster than a hound dog could lick a platter.

One day when I went downtown, I saw a group of students from my school standing in line in front of the movie theater. I had not the foggiest notion why they would be doing that since it was a Loew's Theater, and everybody knew that blacks couldn't go into Loew's Theaters. In Houston, unlike many other cities, blacks didn't even sit in the balcony. As a black you couldn't go into a white theater at all. The blacks had their movie theaters and the whites had theirs.

I walked up to the line of students and saw one of my friends. His name was Wendell Johnson.

He said to me, "Get away, get away, we're doing something here!"

I asked, "What are you doing?"

He said, "We're trying to get tickets to go to this movie theater. We're trying to open it up, desegregate it." That was the first time I heard the word "desegregate."

There they were, and I was insulted. Students from my school were trying to do something as momentous as this without telling me.

I said, "Well, I'm going to stay here too."

They said, "No, you're too little."

I was indignant. Here they were shooing me away because they said I was too little!

They added, "You might get arrested and you don't need to get arrested, so just go away."

I didn't want to disrupt what they were doing so I left. But I never forgot it, and I said to myself that never again would anybody do anything that was socially worthwhile and just leave me out in the cold. Looking back, I believe that episode had a lot to do with my becoming a real activist and agitator for social reform later on in San Francisco in the sixties.

A few months later, eight or ten of us, led by a kid named Anthony Hall, decided to go to a place called Playland Park. This was an amusement park—like a small Coney Island. We were going to try to desegregate it. So we got in various cars, some got on the bus, and we went out there.

Now blacks were allowed in this park only one day a year—and that was the 19th of June, Emancipation Day. But this was not the 19th of June. It was the 23rd of July. In times past, like any other kid, I had loved all the rides, and the cotton candy, and so on. But gradually I realized that being black limited me to one day a year at what I thought was a fabulous place, while whites went there the other 364 days. That just wasn't fair. I felt really cheated.

Anyway, we went to Playland that July day to see if we could get in. We were all prepared to go to jail, if necessary. One of us went up to the ticket booth and asked to buy a ticket while the rest of us waited to see what would happen.

The man in the booth made a phone call to someone. Then a very fat white man came waddling over. He and the ticket seller had a conference for about ten minutes. We expected the police to come, since that's what we thought the phone call was all about. But the police didn't come. And suddenly the first guy went back to his booth and started selling us entry tickets.

We couldn't believe it. We were shocked. And some of us didn't go in because we didn't have any money. We weren't *expecting* to be let in. We figured that the probability of that happening just because we confronted the establishment was zero. What we didn't know at the time was that Playland was going downhill and all these people suddenly wanting to go in was a promise of improved business. For the owner there was a whole new market out there, twenty-five percent of the total market. That was the percentage of the blacks in Houston then. Like any businessperson whose profits were declining, he was looking for new customers, so he took advantage of the available black market.

Actually, we were frustrated and disappointed. We didn't have a chance to picket and then go back and brag about it to our friends. The walls had come tumbling down—but for economic reasons. There was a lesson in that.

On a much larger scale, those same reasons brought an end to most segregation in Houston almost overnight. Houston wanted a major league baseball team, and there was no way for Houston to have such a team without integration. Major league ball owners weren't going to have their star black players sit on the bench if they came to Houston. Those players would have to be able to go to hotels and restaurants and eat with the white players. And so, almost from one day to the next, in 1964, integration came to Houston. One day you couldn't go into W. T. Grant, as I had done, without grabbing your sister and running if she drank from the wrong water fountain. The next day you could drink from any fountain you chose. It didn't matter what the rednecks thought about it. They couldn't do anything. The ones who really counted had made a judgment and said, "This is what we're going to do." And that was it.

Money talks. That's the way it was—and is. For years blacks couldn't, for example, go to Joe's Hash House because Joe owned his own little business and, doggone it, he wasn't going to have any blacks coming into his place and sitting down just like anybody else. But in time that no longer mattered because the major hotels and restaurants—really the finest spots—were the ones that opened up first, not the little hash houses and neighborhood places. And that set a precedent.

When I graduated from high school in January of '62, if anybody had suggested having our senior prom at the Rice Hotel, you would have had the guy's head examined. It would have been insane—like expecting to have a bar mitzvah in Qaddafi's palace.

But only a year and a half later, when my brother graduated, that's what his class did; its graduation exercises were at the Rice Hotel. And suddenly you picked up the newspaper and read that it was possible to go to all the places that had been closed to you. And, in a way, once again you felt cheated. Because if desegregation could be done away with so easily, so quickly, you felt it could have been done away with all along if the right people in town had only decided that was what they wanted.

When I finished high school, I had the option of going to college, and I wanted to go to a good one. I had a girlfriend who was the daughter of a minister, and she was going off to the University of Texas. So I applied to the University of Texas. I had the grades to get in, but I didn't have the money to go to Austin. It would have meant living away from home, and I couldn't afford that. There was another problem, too. At that time, blacks were admitted to the University of Texas only under a court order, and marshals were on campus to make sure that blacks could go to school there in peace and tranquility. Friends of mine in the class ahead of me actually had United States marshals sitting in class with them at UT. That kind of environment did not appeal to me, but since I didn't have the money anyway, it was a theoretical issue.

My only alternative was to go to school in California. There my basic expenses—food and shelter—would be taken care of by my uncle, George Johnson, who lived in San Francisco. He had always said that, since I was "so smart," as he put it, he would educate "that boy." He didn't have any children of his own.

So I went to San Francisco and lived with Uncle George and his wife. They owned an apartment building and, compared to us, they were rich. I applied for admission to the University of San Francisco, to San Francisco State, and to the University of California at Berkeley.

I didn't get into Berkeley; my grades weren't good enough. Competition for that school was fierce. But I did qualify for both San Francisco State and the University of San Francisco. I chose San Francisco State because tuition costs were so low.

So that's how I wound up in California and found myself about to enter college in one of the most colorful cities in the world.

The year was 1962.

A whole new universe was waiting for me.

I told myself that I was ready.

21
Go West, Young Man

In San Francisco, I went to live with Uncle George and his wife. I enrolled in San Francisco State, and a whole new world exploded before my dazzled eyes.

As a young black male in the turbulent sixties, it was inevitable that I would be attracted to the civil rights movement because that's where the action was. With other activist students, some black, some white, I spent a lot of time on picket lines trying to persuade banks and other corporations to hire more minorities. In those days, most of the white activists were Jews. We used to meet sometimes in synagogues to plan our tactics, and it was there that my interest in Judaism was awakened. As I mentioned, my father had shortened his last name to Green so I grew up with that name, but now I changed mine back to Greenberg, after my Russian ancestor. I also took some formal instruction in Judaism—the Reform branch—and began to think of myself as a Jew.

One thing that impressed me about the Jews I met on the picket lines was their courage. In most cases they were the only whites participating. Often they assumed the high-risk jobs, serving as officers and spokesmen for local civil rights groups. This meant they didn't have the anonymity that protected me and others like me. They took significant risks with their careers, their families, and their financial security by being up front on highly controversial issues.

I chose anthropology and international relations as majors at college. The former appealed to me because it involved field work, practical observation of people in action. The latter because I felt it might lead to a career in diplomacy. When I graduated from San Francisco State I was having difficulty finding a job, so I ducked back into the sheltered halls of academe. All my life I've been attracted by the mental stimulus and freedom of expression that you find in a scholastic environment. Eventually, I got my master's degree in public administration and for a while thought seriously of a teaching career. But gradually the lure of law enforcement drew me away from the campus.

The seeds of my interest in being a cop were probably planted in 1968 when I got my first nonacademic job as probation officer in Marin County. After that I helped a friend of mine, Dick Hongisto, run for sheriff of San Francisco County. When he won, I was rewarded with the job of under-sheriff, which I held for fourteen months.

Then I went back to teaching. I had taken a leave of absence from the university when I joined the sheriff's office. I had been teaching part-time, but now I went back full-time. However, I wanted to keep my bridges to the world of law enforcement standing, so I met the requirements for certification as a police officer in California even though I was no longer in the sheriff's department. I taught sociology at Cal State Hayward. Then one day in 1973, I was offered an assistant professorship at the University of North Carolina, and spent two pleasant and stimulating years teaching public administration there.

Actually I was supposed to spend three years at UNC, but I knew that if I was going to make a career of teaching I'd have to work for my PhD, and somehow I had lost interest in more postgraduate study. So I began to send out resumés to various law enforcement agencies, and finally I got an offer from the police department in Corvallis, Oregon. They said they needed a Director of Research and Planning. I wasn't quite sure what that meant. But I knew the University of Oregon was there, where I could probably do some teaching on the side. So I said I'd go. By now it was 1975.

I'd been at Corvallis only a couple of months when I got a call from a friend of mine, David Epstein, whom I'd met in Washington at a convention of law enforcement people. Dave, who was then in Iowa, told me he had just been appointed chief of police in Savannah, Georgia. He figured he was going to need some help and wondered if I would like to join his administrative staff.

I was amazed that Dave Epstein, a PhD from Michigan State, married to a Chinese woman, obviously Jewish himself, could possibly have been selected to handle police affairs in Savannah. I had just come from the South myself, but North Carolina was a very sophisticated university, the Berkeley of the Southeast you might say. I'd always thought of Savannah as a slow-moving, sleepy Southern city, living dreamily in the nineteenth century. I thought Dave had lost his mind.

Still, I didn't put him off altogether. I told him it

would take about six months for me to get my job
under control in Corvallis. Then maybe I'd call him
back.

Lo and behold, five months later he called me again,
this time from Savannah. By now it was the spring of
1976. I finally told Dave I'd fly down and talk about
the job.

I remember flying into Savannah in early April, just
as the trees were turning green. I was amazed at the
almost total lack of skyscrapers; Savannah seemed like
a very small city. I was also amazed when the man they
sent to meet me, Major Jim Weaver of the Savannah
Police Department, reached over and took my bags
when they came off the airplane. A white major carrying the bags of a black guy getting off a plane from
Oregon? This didn't quite fit in with my expectations
of Savannah. Moreover, they could have sent any
number of flunkies to meet me, but this was the number
two man, right next to the Chief. I was impressed. I
spent a lot of time talking to Weaver and Epstein and
the city manager, Don Mendonsa. Finally, I said I would
come, but that I'd need a couple of months to wind up
things in Corvallis.

I remember one little event in Savannah that gave a
salutary jolt to my ego. I had answered a call to some
minor traffic accident, and the man involved kept calling me "Officer." Officer this and officer that. Finally
I said to him, a bit haughtily, "I'm not *Officer* Greenberg.
I'm *Major* Greenberg."

He stared at me, and for a moment I thought he
was going to burst out laughing. "Well, lah-de-dah!" he
said. "Laaah-dee daaah! *Major* Greenberg!"

It was a long time before I tried to impress anyone
else with my exalted sense of my own importance!

One of the things I had to leave behind in Corvallis
was a part-time job teaching at Oregon State. It was an

introductory course in political science, and I hated to give that up, but I figured there would be similar opportunities later.

There were about 230 men and women in the Savannah Police Department at that time, and I'm sure some of the less educated rank and file got a severe shock when a black turned up as a major. They were willing to concede that blacks should have some advancement, but only to the ranks of corporal or sergeant, though I think they did have one black lieutenant when I arrived. So I was prepared for some unspoken resistance, but it didn't bother me since I had the support of Chief Epstein and City Manager Mendonsa. And most people were prepared to wait and see how I handled the job before making any final judgments. Being single in those days, I was able to ride in patrol cars a lot at night, which I liked, and gradually I got to know the officers and won their confidence and support.

Dave Epstein stayed about five years in Savannah before moving on. He did an excellent job. I stayed about three years, until 1979.

One very valuable lesson I learned in Savannah came from Dave Epstein. It had to do with crowd control. Dave taught me that the most effective weapon a police officer has in dealing with unruly or dangerous crowds is the *individual* in that crowd who is capable of leading them one way or another. If you can make that individual do what you want, then the situation won't explode out of control.

I remember one hot, sultry Sunday afternoon at the corner of Gwinnett and Habersham streets in Savannah. An angry crowd of blacks had gathered outside a supermarket. Some grievance, real or imagined, had inflamed them against the police. It looked like a riot in the making, and Epstein and I and a bunch of other cops had gone down to deal with it. We had tear gas and

we had backup forces just out of sight. We were ready
for anything.

One enraged black guy was shaking his finger in
Epstein's face and yelling all sorts of accusations about
police brutality and so on. The chief just stood there,
taking all the abuse without turning a hair. The crowd
was egging on the big black guy. The whole situation
looked very ugly to me. If this fellow could talk to the
chief like that and get away with it, what would he have
to say to a major like myself? I wanted to deal with
him. I wanted to shake him up. I said to Epstein, "Do
you want me to grab this guy?" I was more than ready
to do it.

Epstein just shook his head. He kept listening to the
barrage of verbal abuse until the guy began to repeat
himself. Then the chief calmly put his arm around the
man's shoulders and said, "Let's move off by ourselves
and have a little talk." The guy looked amazed, but he
went along with the chief. What Epstein said to him I
don't know, probably some promise that the episode
that had caused all the trouble wouldn't be repeated.
Anyway, they soon came back. The big black fellow
(who by now was a hero to the crowd) said loudly,
"Okay, I'm going to hold you to that!" They shook
hands. Then the black guy turned to the others. "Go
on home!" he said. And they all went home.

Epstein always used to say, "Don't sweat the small
stuff." In this case, the small stuff was his own ego, his
own pride. He simply put that aside; he had a more
important objective in view. He knew what he wanted,
and he got it. I never forgot that.

Dave Epstein was—and still is—a cop with a rare
ability to put himself in the other fellow's shoes. I remember another occasion when an angry crowd had
gathered on a sweltering afternoon. "You know what
the solution to this is?" Epstein said to me. "It's not

force. It's not tear gas. It's air conditioners. Give me three hundred window units to put in these poor devils' houses and they'll simply disappear. They're out here on the street because their miserable homes are too hot for an animal to stay in, much less a human being." He was right about that, too.

Probably the most important thing that happened to me during my tour of duty in Savannah was a deepening of my interest in Judaism. Up until then, 1976, I had been a nominal Jew, going to synagogue, taking some instruction, and so on. In Savannah I began to be involved in a more profound, more theological way. It came about like this.

There was a cantor at Agudath Achim, the Conservative synagogue on Lee Boulevard, who usually walked to Friday night services. As he walked along one evening, Cantor Radzik was approached by a man and woman who asked him for money. Of course, being a very religious Jew, he didn't have any money since he was walking to Sabbath services. Enraged because he had no money, the couple beat him quite badly. It turned out that a few weeks before a rabbi visiting Savannah had also been attacked and beaten by a couple. We in the police department believed that both incidents involved the same two persons.

When he heard that the cantor had been attacked, Chief Epstein naturally was concerned. He asked me if I would escort Cantor Radzik for a few weeks as he walked to Friday night services.

I had attended that synagogue myself on several occasions and knew the cantor. I agreed to meet him at his house and walk the two miles or so between there and the synagogue. After services, we would walk back. During these walks we became good friends, and it became a regular Friday night routine—which meant that I had the added benefit of attending services every

Friday without fail. We would walk and talk and discuss various types of political, social, and religious issues. These walks lasted for more than two years.

Cantor Radzik was a remarkable man. Born in Poland, he had survived concentration camps there. Cantor Radzik had been trained as a rabbi as well as a cantor, and often had to function in both roles because rabbis kept coming and going at this particular synagogue. The congregation had a saying: "If he's no good, we'll fire him; if he's any good, he won't stay." Undoubtedly that was true. As a result, Cantor Radzik had outlasted four or five rabbis.

Which was fortunate for me, because as my walks with Cantor Radzik progressed, I actually began serious instruction for the purpose of conversion. We went at this for quite a long while. The cantor would recommend books for me to read. I would read them and we would discuss them on our walks. It was a fascinating reintroduction to Jewish philosophical thought and philosophy. Before then, my relationship to Judaism had been a sort of superficial, ephemeral thing. But thanks to Cantor Radzik, it developed into a serious effort at study and interaction with the Jewish community. It was a very enjoyable and unique way—a kind of one-on-one dialogue, really—of learning about the basic dynamics of Judaism and Jewish thought and philosophy.

One evening after I had been in Savannah about three years, I had a call from Don McKenna, the newly appointed city manager of Opa Locka, Florida. He was from Bucks County, Pennsylvania, originally, but now he had taken this job in the town of Opa Locka, near Miami, where he hoped to accomplish all sorts of marvelous reforms. He had heard of me through the International City Management Association. I had an appli-

cation on file there for a job as police chief somewhere.
Don had fired his police chief for insubordination, and
he wanted to know if I might be interested in the job.
I wasn't really interested, but there was something very
persuasive about Don McKenna, so at last I said I'd
come down and take a look.

What I found myself looking at was not very impres-
sive. Originally, Opa Locka had been a planned city
with an Arabian theme—the City Hall looked like an
Arabian palace out in the desert somewhere—but now
it obviously was going downhill. The population was
about fifty percent black, mostly poor. The whites were
mostly elderly and poor also. It certainly didn't look
very promising to me, but it did represent a challenge.
Where the police force was concerned, there was
nowhere to go but up. I found there were more lawsuits
pending against the police for alleged use of excessive
force and denial of constitutional rights than there were
men on the force. I think there were twenty-seven officers and twenty-eight suits pending. Not a sign of very
high efficiency or morale!

The only really good thing about Opa Locka was the
City Manager, Don McKenna. This highly qualified
white guy, who could have had his pick of much easier
and more rewarding jobs, was willing to knock himself
out in an effort to help the poor black citizens of Opa
Locka. And the poor white citizens too. He really cared,
and when you talked to him some of his enthusiasm
rubbed off on you. So in the end I agreed to serve as
chief of police in Opa Locka, and in 1979 I said good-
bye to my Savannah friends.

The job in Opa Locka was followed by two tours of
duty in Florida, one in Orlando and another in Tallahassee. I didn't forget my friends in Savannah, though,
and used to go back to see them once in a while. On
one such visit from Orlando a very important encounter

took place. I met a goodlooking college professor named Sara Horne. Perhaps I need a separate chapter to tell you about that meeting and how—as the saying goes—I chased her until she caught me.

22

The Confirmed Bachelor
Succumbs

One Christmas I had gone by train from Orlando to
Savannah to see a girlfriend. I love to ride trains. I
don't care where I go, if I have the time and the option
I'll ride the train. If it's a steam train, all the better.

I was on my way back, and just before the train
pulled out of the Savannah station early in the morning
I saw an unusually attractive lady get on board. There
was something about her, and not just her good looks,
that intrigued me. And so, as the train began to move
through the flat Georgia pinelands, I went looking for
her. When I found her I said good morning, and we
talked a bit. Finally I asked her if she'd have breakfast
with me in the dining car.

I didn't know it at the time, but Sara Horne had
never been on a train before. She had been on plenty
of planes but never on a train. She was teaching
mathematics at the University of Northern Iowa. Sara
was a native of Savannah, home for the Christmas holi-

days, and she had decided to visit some friends in Florida, about an hour's drive from Orlando. The train was the easiest way to get there. When I asked her to have breakfast with me, she thought we'd just get a snack out of some coin machine. She had no idea there was such a thing as a dining car. She thought riding the train was like being on a bus, only with a lot of buses in a row.

So when we came to the dining car and Sara saw real sit-down tables with real cloth napkins and table silver and flowers and so on, she was very impressed. We sat down and we didn't just eat, we dined. We dined and we talked, and in almost no time, it seemed, we were in Orlando. I had a chance to meet the people who were picking Sara up. They suggested I might drive over and visit them in the next couple of days. I said, "Of course," and I really meant it. I found that I could hardly wait to get over there.

It's amazing how quickly an attraction can spring up between two people when the chemistry is right. When Sara went back to Iowa, we began writing a lot of letters and making a great many phone calls. I told her to call me collect whenever she felt like it, not knowing that the women of Savannah hold the all-time international record for telephone loquacity. Pretty soon I began to think it might be cheaper to marry the lady than go on with these extended conversations.

Sara made three trips to Orlando, allegedly to see her relatives, but actually to see me. On the first of these visits we went to Disney World, where, memorably, we exchanged our first kiss. The second time she brought me some cookies she said she had made. They were absolutely sensational; no cookies she has made since ever lived up to those. On her third visit Sara said a bit plaintively she had decided that I was too much of a confirmed bachelor for her to have a chance.

This revelation of her innermost feelings finally prompted me to go out and buy a ring. I had it in my hand when I asked her to marry me. She said yes. That was in August of 1980.

Of course, as soon as she said yes I began to have terrible qualms. Sara was a wonderful person, outgoing, gregarious, at ease with everyone, but marriage to her or anyone began to seem so *final*. When she quit her job in Iowa and moved back to Georgia, my feet got colder than ever. But it was too late. In December we went to San Francisco to be married at city hall, just before I was to start my new job in Tallahassee.

We wanted—I wanted—a private ceremony performed by a judge. A Jewish judge. That's what I got. Sara wanted to have the reception in Savannah to introduce me to all her friends. I didn't want a reception, all that fluff and expense and so on. Sara said, "Never mind; I'll pay for it. All you have to do is be there." So she did. And I was.

Sara had a hard time finding a place for the reception on the date in question. Then she got a bright idea: to see if the social hall of the synagogue was available. I can only cringe when I think of the shock that the clerk who answered the synagogue's telephone must have felt as Sara described the wedding reception and all of the "traif"—the nonkosher food, such as ham—she wanted to bring. Fortunately, to the relief of both the clerk and myself, the social hall was not available on that day.

Sara had no knowledge at all then about what to expect at a Jewish wedding reception and what could be brought to a Jewish facility. In her mind, she was planning a Baptist wedding reception in a Jewish social hall. Years later, when she had learned better, we would laugh at the lack of knowledge about my religion she had had then.

Now I was a married man, but the bachelor side of me died hard. At least I wasn't in the same class as another confirmed bachelor who, after the wedding guests had departed, turned to his bride and said, "Alone at last—except, of course, for you." Still, one little episode that happened about a month after we were married proved that I had not yet fully succumbed. Sara and I went to a supermarket in Tallahassee and each of us wandered off pushing different carts in search of this item or that. At one point, when her cart became rather crowded, Sara put several items in my cart. When I finished, I was so utterly used to doing my own shopping and putting the groceries in the car and driving away that that was exactly what I did, completely forgetting that my bride of a month was still in the store.

It wasn't until I began unpacking the groceries and found myself frowning over items I didn't remember buying that suddenly a blinding light went on in my head: Sara! I rushed back to the store and found her sitting on the curb with an unfathomable look on her face. I was so embarrassed that I gave her no explanation at all, just drove home in a somewhat strained silence. Later we talked and laughed about it, but it showed me what a powerful thing habit is.

Like all married couples, Sara and I differ in many ways. I'm Jewish. She's Baptist—sings in her church choir. This is no problem for either of us. I go to hear her sing sometimes. Sometimes she comes to synagogue with me. Neither of us would dream of trying to convert the other. If and when we have children, that won't be a problem either: we'll let them become familiar with both religions and then make their own choice.

Sara, who comes from a close-knit family in Savannah, is constantly surprised and even a bit troubled because I have so few contacts with members of my own family. One reason, I tell her, may be that I had such ultraclose contacts with my brothers when we were growing up. Four of us not only shared one room, we shared the same bed. That bed was divided into quarters, and each of us jealously guarded his quarter. We even drew lines of demarcation on the headboard. When you are one of four growing boys sleeping in the same bed, you don't have to worry about close family ties. You have them every night.

In spite of such minor differences, there are plenty of major areas where Sara and I agree. We agree, for example, that what is needed most in the black community today is a breakthrough on the cultural and educational fronts. The battle against discrimination and segregation has been fought, and to a large extent it has been won. By now we should have moved on from there. Yet we are not moving on.

Take sports, for example. Certainly in the last two decades black athletes have come to dominate most sports, and that can be a source of satisfaction and pride. But I think we may have overdone it. At this very moment there are hundreds of thousands, maybe millions, of young black men bouncing a basketball somewhere on a concrete slab because they see a handful of professional athletes making enormous salaries and becoming household words. Naturally, every kid bouncing a basketball thinks he may become such a star. But the odds against that happening are enormous. Statistically, that same kid would have a better chance of becoming a U.S. senator than he would of being picked up by a top pro team.

Sports have become a deadly siren song for millions of young black men. Even among the handful who succeed in making it to the big time, few are equipped educationally, psychologically, or socially to deal with that kind of success. What poor person, regardless of color or background, is prepared to deal suddenly with an income of a million or more dollars a year? The results are often tragic.

It's my belief that no ethnic group, no racial group, can fulfill its destiny, or rise to great heights, by throwing a basketball around or hitting a baseball over a fence. That's not the fabric that great civilizations are made of. For my part, I would take every black football star, every black basketball star, every black baseball star and trade them all for a hundred really qualified teachers of biology, chemistry, and algebra in the schools.

Look at other minorities that have bypassed sports, for the most part, and yet achieved great things. The Jews come instantly to mind. During the 1920s and 1930s, most Jewish newspapers in New York didn't even have a sports section. I have little patience with black parents who object when higher academic standards are required for student athletes. They are afraid these stricter rules may deprive their kids of a crucial after-school career in sports. I couldn't give two hoots in hell whether any of those kids ever picked up a basketball or not. I want them to pick up the test tube and the compass. We blacks have already demonstrated that we can surpass other racial groups when it comes to sports. We don't need to keep on doing that. We need to develop the cultural, the intellectual, the scientific values required to succeed in a modern technological environment. We need to develop more Duke Ellingtons, more Marian Andersons, more Ralph Bunches, more Thurgood Marshalls, more André Wattses, more Robert McNairs. We need to help our people discover that these are the important things, the things that matter, not the frantic rat race for supremacy in sports.

Another subject Sara and I often discuss is the enormous problem of illegitimate births among black teenagers. Even as recently as 1960, seventy-five percent of black children were raised in two-parent homes. I remember that when I was a kid, to be illegitimate was considered a real stigma. People gave up their children for adoption in order to spare the children the shame of illegitimacy. I remember the whispers: So-and-So had to drop out of school because she was pregnant. It was a source of acute embarrassment. People pointed out those girls, snickered behind their backs, considered them immoral, shunned them. Now such pregnancies are so common that if a sociologist from Mars took a look at our society he might think he was observing the old Samoan culture in which the identity of the father was of no consequence. None at all.

Furthermore, the economic outlook for those illegitimate babies is worse than bleak. Their mothers have very limited earning power. The children are born into a situation from which it's almost impossible to escape. These young black mothers, trapped in an increasingly technological society, are literally breeding themselves into poverty because the social sanctions against such activities have broken down.

Perhaps some day the pendulum will begin to swing back from total permissiveness to some sort of rules of conduct imposed and endorsed by a society that, after all, cannot really wish to sit by and watch itself commit suicide.

But it is a disheartening and frightening situation.

A few months after Sara and I were married, my mother died. I missed her terribly; I still do. While she lived she was the focal point of our whole family. Everyone kept in close touch with her. She acted as liaison and news-gatherer for the rest of us. She was always disappointed that we did not take her lead and share things more or have greater interaction with one another. She was one of the most gregarious people I have ever known. She could get along with anybody. When she died in 1981, the central focus in our lives was gone.

She used to visit with each of us for about two weeks every year wherever we were living around the country. Whenever she would visit with me, we would go on long drives through the country. She loved to stop at antique shops to browse. In the evenings I would barbecue steaks and she would make peach ice cream for the two of us.

I think I inherited my love of reading from my mother. She would read anything, even advertising signs along the street or newspaper classifieds. When we were young children, we could never understand why she read those ads when we all knew that often she did not have even a dollar in her purse.

What turned out to be our first and only photograph with her and all the rest of us, except Donald, who had been killed in Vietnam, was taken at Carolyn's house in the spring of 1981. She died shortly after that. My father still lives in Houston.

Mama's death was a great loss to us all. She was, in effect, our family. We were so unaccustomed to getting along without her that it was years after her death before we spoke about her in the past tense.

Sara and I were in Tallahassee for about a year and a half. My job there was deputy to my good friend Pat Gallagher, Director of Police Standards of Training for the state of Florida. But I wasn't really happy; it seemed to me that at the state level of law enforcement you mainly give speeches and shuffle papers. You don't have the active, firsthand involvement that you have at the local level.

A major turning point in my life came in 1982 when we heard that John F. Conroy, the much admired and respected police chief of Charleston had died. It was a terrific shock to everybody. John had accomplished wonders in eliminating inefficiency and racism and corruption from Charleston's police force. It was hard to see how he could be replaced at all.

When I heard that applications were being taken for a successor, I decided to toss my hat into the ring. I didn't really think a black applicant would have a chance in "the cradle of the Confederacy," much less a black Jewish applicant who came from outside the state.

But I sent in my resumé anyway, giving Pat Gallagher and one or two others as references. Finally word came back that the field had been narrowed to six finalists. And to my amazement the black Jewish outsider was one of the six.

23
The War That Wasn't

When the call came in 1982 from the mayor's office in Charleston asking me to appear for an interview for the job of chief of police, I never thought for a moment that I would actually get it. Although I was qualified, I knew that other qualified people were being considered. I was just one more applicant. I also knew that it would take considerable courage on the part of the appointing official—I didn't even know who he was—to choose a black man as head of the police department in a city like Charleston.

I was told that black people in the community had gone to the mayor and asked him to consider the possibility of appointing a qualified black as chief of police. Of course they knew that such a person would have to come from outside Charleston, probably outside South Carolina. I think the black leaders felt that relations between the police and the black community still needed improvement and that perhaps even the *consideration* of appointing a black could improve the climate. They probably told themselves a black would have no real chance, but just including one in the list of finalists would help.

I knew myself that my chances had to be slim. Certainly being a Jew could not be expected to help. Whatever prejudices people may have toward Jews, they readily transfer to a black who is Jewish. And there was another consideration, too: the importance of the job itself. When a city chooses a chief of police, that city is saying, Look, we are placing the lives and safety of our citizens and the security of their property in your hands. That means there is no such thing as a "token" police chief. You can have a token member of some minority on the city council, or the state legislature, or even a token judge, but there is no token chief of police. It is a job of enormous importance and responsibility. I didn't think that Charleston, the city that fired the first shot in the war between the states, was ready to make a commitment like that. Not to anyone with a black skin.

But I was wrong. The city council in Charleston has twelve members. They voted unanimously to hire me. Unanimously! A lot of people were amazed. They were flabbergasted. They were stunned. The ones who took a dim view of my appointment consoled themselves with the thought that I wouldn't last six months. I would go down. I would fail. The whole thing just wouldn't work.

I was braced for Klansmen parading around City Hall when the time came for me to be sworn in, as had happened shortly before in Houston when Lee Brown, a black friend of mine, was sworn in as chief of police there. I didn't know then that Charlestonians would never be so graceless, so primitive, so barbaric as to permit a rabble-rousing group of that kind to challenge the authority of those who had decided to appoint a black police chief.

I have since come to know that Charleston is completely different from the rest of the South. But I didn't know it then. I had no idea of the grace and stability of this little city. It was a city that had not suffered the dislocation and bitterness that virtually every other Southern city went through during the civil rights movement in the late fifties and sixties. It was no better than the others in its treatment of minorities, but it was much better—indeed it was outstanding—in its realization that times were changing, that old injustices had to be rectified, that enlightened leadership could do it.

So I came into town with my guard up, ready for a bruising uphill battle. I would make a fight of it, all right, but I thought I might lose. I knew I had certain things going for me. My predecessor, Chief John F. Conroy, had done a sensational job in turning the police department around. His skills, his understanding, his patience had been extraordinary. I was to benefit enormously from the years of work and dedication he had brought to the department. And there were certain other symbolic things in my favor. The oath of office was to be administered by a fellow black: Chief Municipal Judge Arthur McFarland. Rabbi Alan Cohen was to give the invocation and the benediction at the ceremony. The mostly white city council had already given me unanimous approval. It was as if the black community and the Jewish community and a substantial proportion of the white Christian community were saying, Let's give him a shot. Let's give ol' Reub a shot.

But the thing that made the deepest impression on me was a gesture from a lady, Alice Conroy, widow of John Conroy, who might easily have been expected to have some reservations about the stranger who was coming into town to take over her late husband's job and try to fill his shoes. I was so sure that this would be her attitude, and the attitude of the other members of the former chief's family, that I was uncomfortable even at the thought of meeting them. I assumed at best we would share a polite nod and a cool hello, no more than that.

I needed a place to stay temporarily in Charleston until I found a permanent home. So I asked someone in the city planning department to see what might be available. Back came word that Alice Conroy had a carriage house that she usually rented to visitors to Charleston's Spoleto Festival. But Spoleto was still four or five weeks away, and Alice Conroy had sent word that she would be very happy for me to stay there temporarily.

This offer just left me stunned. I had never met Alice. All she knew about me was what she had read in the paper. Yet here she was asking me to come and stay in her carriage house. No other welcome mat, no other red carpet, could possibly have had as much significance. If Alice Conroy asked me to stay in her home, why worry about anybody else?

So I came to her house, and she introduced herself and showed me around. It was a very old antebellum house, just loaded with tradition and history. There was an ancient fireplace in the room where I spent the first night, and in my mind's eye I could visualize the workers, probably black, probably slaves, who had laid those bricks, whose patient hands had sanded down and oiled those floorboards of South Carolina heart-of-pine. I thought of how incomprehensible it would have been to them, how impossible for them to conceive in their wildest dreams, that a black would ever sleep here, let alone one who was now chief of police of the city. I didn't see all this as a negative thing; I felt no bitterness about the past. I just felt somehow special and privileged to be within these walls, to be in this gracious old city. And I knew I would do everything I could not to disappoint the hopes and dreams of those who had laid the brick and mortar of the fireplace and with their primitive hand tools had fashioned the very boards under my feet.

That gesture by Alice Conroy really changed my attitude completely. I had come into town with sword drawn, guard up. I was ready to fight dragons in the form of sheeted Klansmen. I was ready to charge like Don Quixote against the windmills of racism. Now I found myself remembering what the flower children had said back in San Francisco in the 1960s: What if they gave a war and nobody came?

Well, here I was in Charleston, braced for war.

And nobody came.

After I'd been chief of police in Charleston for about three years, CBS sent Morley Safer down to interview me for "Sixty Minutes." I suppose the producers thought a black (and Jewish) police chief in an old patrician Southern town like Charleston was newsworthy. They probably checked and found that crime statistics in Charleston were down. Anyway, they came. I was featured in one of three sections of the show in January of 1986, so I had only about ten or fifteen minutes on camera—but those few minutes were like a bombshell.

There were no rehearsals. Safer just tossed questions at me and I answered as honestly as I could. I said that punishment—jail—is the best way to stop someone from pursuing a life of crime, and I added that the only effective remedy where such criminals are concerned is time. If you looked at prison statistics, I said, you'd see that the number of people arrested, even long-time criminals, for a crime committed after the age of 35 is very small. The recklessness, the willingness to take chances, just aren't there.

"So what do we do?" Safer asked. "Take the habitual 23-year-old criminal and lock him up until he's 35?"

"Well," I said dryly, "I certainly wouldn't parole any of them!"

Safer also asked me about black-on-black crime. I said that since most victims of crime were black, blacks had the most urgent reason to want crime controlled. I added that in my opinion blacks should stop using racism as an excuse for antisocial behavior by other blacks. If a black teenager knocked down an elderly black woman, broke her arm, and stole her purse, where was the element of racism in that? I said that it made no sense to me to argue that the mugger was the way he was because of discrimination; he was the way he was because he chose to be that way.

I wanted to make other comments as well. For instance, the widespread legal custom of granting probation for a first offense—what's the point of that? It just gives the juvenile crook a license to commit his first crime. If he knows there will be no punishment, why should he hesitate? Or the whole system of plea bargaining that waters down sentences until they don't even remotely fit the crime. But we ran out of time.

A lot of viewers just seized pen and paper while the show was still on and fired off a letter agreeing with me, including, surprisingly, a great many lawyers. Out of all the mail I received, only one letter expressed disagreement, and that came from a sociologist who thought I was being too simplistic and too hard on crooks. If logic is simplistic, then I guess simplistic is what I am. As for being tough on criminals, I took that as a compliment.

There's no doubt about it, those few minutes on

prime time television shoved me into the national spot-light, and, like it or not, I've been there ever since. I've had more speaking invitations than I can count, more job offers, more opportunities to travel all over the country—indeed all over the world—and give my opinions on crime control. I consider myself a very fortunate fellow.

And now perhaps the time has come to try to answer a question that I'm asked about ten times a day, or so it seems: "Why are you a Jew?"

24
Why I Am a Jew

"Why did you decide to become a Jew?" I have come to accept the question as inevitable. People want to know. "How did you happen to choose Judaism as your religion out of all religions?" they ask.

The plain and clearly observable fact that I am also black raises, in the minds of many people, an inconsistency of puzzling proportions. "How can you be *both* black and Jewish? Are you crazy? Now you are going to be discriminated against twice!"

This notion that a black Jew is going to be doubly discriminated against can be put to rest quickly. I consider myself no worse and no better off for having adopted the Jewish religion than I would have been had I adopted any other religion. I am Jewish. I am black. Almost all of the people who hate blacks also hate Jews. So I gain virtually no more enemies or detractors by being Jewish than I would have had anyway as a black person.

There was no specific moment when I decided to become a practicing Jew. It happened over a period of years, the result of many influences. As I mentioned, I did not start using my grandfather's name, Greenberg, until I was in college; my father had shortened it to Green, and that was the name all of us children used when we were growing up in Houston. I knew my grandfather was a Jew, of course. I think perhaps that fact penetrated and remained in my unconscious mind, and thus the roots of motivation existed for the adoption of the name and ultimately of the Jewish faith.

In addition, the secular experiences with Jews in my youth in Houston and later with Jews in San Francisco were important external influences. Had I never become involved in the civil rights movement of the 1960s, it is not likely that I would have adopted the faith of my grandfather. When I arrived in San Francisco to attend college in 1962, I was not committed to any particular faith, but I was not an atheist or even an agnostic. I had always believed in the existence of a supreme being, and gradually I began to feel that Judaism might offer me a way to approach that being with dignity and reverence.

The civil rights movement in San Francisco, and in perhaps most other urban areas outside the South, was almost as much a Jewish movement as it was a black movement. At that time, equal access to public accommodations was the big issue. Like blacks, as a minority group, Jews had problems gaining access to public accommodations, housing, employment, club membership, and so on. It was both natural and, given the history of the Jews, logical for Jews to be involved in civil rights projects in proportions far exceeding their ratio to the overall population. It was no accident that two of the three civil rights activists killed in Mississippi

were Jews. The murders of Andrew Goodman and
Michael Schwerner were as much the result of their
being Jews as James Chaney's murder was of his being
black.

With so many Jews in the forefront of the civil rights
movement, it was only natural that, when we needed
places to meet to plan our efforts against discrimination
in jobs, housing, schools, and other areas, we often met
at various synagogues. We met most frequently at the
Beth Shalom Synagogue in San Francisco, where Rabbi
Saul White served. This was my very first really mean-
ingful contact wih the Jewish religion, although I had
known Jewish people all my life.

These meetings, tumultuous at times even though
they were held in and around synagogues, made a deep
impression on me. I saw young men and women argu-
ing with rabbis. Rabbis, while certainly respected in both
religious and secular matters, still accepted critical feed-
back from their congregants. My personal observation
of Christian churches is that, for the most part, if a
congregant does not approve of a sermon or other view
expressed by a priest or minister, he or she simply
ignores it, or changes churches. In Judaism I learned
that if you don't agree with the rabbi's sermon or counsel, you let him know it, and the sooner the better. The
argument or complaint is presented in such a manner
that one's appreciation and respect for the rabbi is in
no way diminished. If a line of Christians waited outside
a priest's or minister's office to complain about a sermon, it would be considered most unusual, almost a
crisis. Should Jews line up at the door of a rabbi's study
to argue a point, it would be the norm.

This free exchange of ideas is one of the basic qual-
ities that attracted me to Judaism. Here was a religion
where dissent and cooperation were both encouraged

and expected. What's more, this religion has survived for thousands of years not in spite of its uninhibited exchange of opinions but primarily because of it.

Another thing that I found attractive about Judaism was that as a religion it had nothing to sell. If you want what Judaism has to offer, you are welcome to adopt it, but no one is going to come calling to persuade you to try it out. Unlike most religions, Judaism does not claim that you have to accept it in order to be happy, live in peace, or go to heaven. It makes no requirement that you believe anything, except in a supreme being. It only requires that you agree to live in peace and not molest your fellow man.

To me, this is one of the greatest benefits of Judaism. The most ironic paradox I know is that so many of the other religions will not permit to Jews what Judaism permits to each of them. Many Christians, and Moslems too, proclaim that theirs is the only religion in which a person can find salvation. Judaism is different. In the *Bible* you find, for example, that to lead a good life there is no requirement that a person be Jewish. People don't have to be Jews to be virtuous.

Judaism teaches absolute equality. No one is better than anyone else. It also teaches charity: a Jew must not ignore the suffering of others. These and other laws are not just religious precepts. They must govern all of your life—your business life, your family life, "thy going out and thy coming in."

As a law enforcement officer, I especially value Judaism's emphasis on personal responsibility. There is no such excuse as "I was a victim of circumstances." You must say a flat no to unethical and unlawful behavior and take full responsibility for your own actions.

From the start I was impressed, too, by Judaism's emphasis on ethical behavior in human relationships.

In the civil rights movement, we used to have heated debates on the propriety of certain tactics that we used on the picket lines. Rabbi White, who was just as strong an advocate of civil rights as the rest of us, always spoke up when he thought we were getting out of bounds and becoming guilty of harassment to an unfair or unwise degree.

For example, we wanted a bank that had very few minority employees to hire more. To get their attention, we would wait in line for the teller, then ask for change of a twenty dollar bill in pennies and then stand there and count them. We figured this would disrupt the normal flow of business, which it certainly did. I remember Rabbi White pointing out calmly but emphatically that, while this might annoy the bank officials, it could hardly fail to infuriate other customers backed up behind us. Thus we would do more harm than good to the civil rights movement. Time and again he brought us back into line. I realize now that his attitude was based on the cornerstone of Judaism that is expressed so well in the Talmudic anecdote about the Rabbi Hillel. A Gentile came to the Rabbi Hillel and said to him scornfully, "I will convert if you can teach me all of Judaism while I stand on one foot." The Rabbi replied, "What is offensive to you, do not do to others. That is the essence of Judaism. The rest is commentary. Now go and study."

I have mentioned that Sara and I were in Tallahassee for only a year and a half. It was not a very productive period as far as my career was concerned, but those eighteen months made a major contribution to my basic spiritual development.

It was in Tallahassee that I became involved with a group of young Jewish families that had split off from a Reform synagogue to start a Conservative congregation of their own, Shromre Torah. My earlier contacts had been with Reform Judaism in San Francisco, and hese led eventually to instruction and conversion. I have to admit, though, that while involvement in the Reform movement was an interesting experience, and while I fully appreciate that Reform Judaism meets the spiritual needs of many dedicated Jews, it left me, at the core of my being, unmoved. For me, it was more like a seminar in graduate school than a profoundly life-changing experience. I think it was inevitable that, seeking a deeper and more demanding religious expression, I would become interested in the Conservative movement sooner or later. Eventually that is what happened, beginning in 1976 in Savannah. As I mentioned earlier, I took serious instruction for the purpose of formal conversion with Cantor Radzik during the two years I walked with him to synagogue every Friday night.

To my mind, the Conservative movement is what Judaism really is: the middle way. Too much of anything, too much pleasure or too much suffering, can be bad. Nothing to excess. In San Francisco, back in the sixties, the Reform movement tended to be on the left wing of social reform. The Conservative movement was much closer to the center.

On the other hand, the Orthodox movement was too restrictive for me. I understand that the spiritual needs of millions of Jews can be completely fulfilled only by the unalterable traditions of Orthodoxy. For me, however, there was no point in pretending that I would be able to keep kosher. There was no point in agreeing that I would not drive a car on the Sabbath or go to the movies on my day of rest. I knew from the beginning that the level of commitment I had was not sufficient to make such choices possible, let alone imperative, for me. The Conservative movement indeed required sincere dedication, but it was not a restrictive form of dedication, and eventually I decided that here was where I belong for the rest of my life as a Jew.

I have always been welcomed at Jewish congregations. This was especially so at Reform and Conservative congregations, though a few people wanted to know about the validity of my conversion before they were willing to shake my hand. When I was single, some even suspected that I was really in the congregation in quest of a wife. In fact, one lady tried to get me to date her daughter, finally saying that even though I was black she considered me a *nice* black Jewish boy and found me more acceptable than the Catholic boy her daughter was dating.

By far the deepest emotional reaction I have ever had to being both black and Jewish came during a visit to Israel in 1986. The joy of being Jewish consumed me as it must all Jews on ascending into the City of Jerusalem. The pride of being black had been instilled in me in countless ways by my parents. And at the Ethiopian Absorption Center in Israel, the twain met.

I will never forget the faces of the Ethiopian Jewish children and their parents. There were about forty of these black Jews, the largest number I had ever seen gathered in one place. It was, however, neither their number nor their blackness that so moved me. It was the realization that these people had survived in Africa as dedicated Jews for thousands of years, cut off from their fellow Jews, under the harshest of social and physical conditions. Now here they were in Israel, over sixteen thousand of them. And they had been sought out and welcomed by a predominantly white and Western-oriented country. They had been rescued by other Jews in a series of dramatic airlifts. I remember thinking that in the past the only times a white country had brought out blacks from the continent of Africa was as slaves. Yet now tiny and beleaguered Israel had brought them home as full-fledged citizens. Whatever difficulties there may be for them down the road, the Falashas—the Ethiopian Jews—were welcomed warmly, as are all Jews in Israel.

As I stood there watching them, I was proud, tremendously proud of being what I am—a Jew.

25
A First-Class Crime-Fighting Machine

Now that I've told you something about myself, perhaps it's time to say a few words about the men and women who make up one of the most effective crime-control units in the nation: the Charleston Police Department.

Let me begin with a question: what does the public have a right to expect from its blue-uniformed guardians? First of all, protection. Protection from robbers, rapists, muggers, purse snatchers—all the antisocial elements that threaten law-abiding people with loss of property or bodily harm.

People want their police to be available quickly when needed. They would like these officers to be caring human beings, capable of feeling genuine concern for the victims of a crime. They want them to be fair-minded, free of bigotry, incapable of abusing the authority that comes with the job.

They want their police force to be made up of men and women who are emotionally stable, in control of themselves at all times. They expect them to be brave in the face of danger, able to handle themselves in a fight, skilled in the use of firearms but reluctant to use them.

They hope the men and women in blue will be intelligent, capable of making fast, accurate decisions, thoroughly familiar with the laws and statutes they may be called upon to enforce. They want them to be incorruptible, impervious to bribes, incapable of favoritism in their dealings with the public.

They would like to see the members of their police force well paid, partly because they know the hazards of the job are great, partly because they are aware that low pay means low morale and low morale means poor performance.

Above all, these typical citizens would like to believe that the police are their friends and allies, so that if they see a patrol car cruise by their house they will feel a sense of reassurance, and if a uniformed officer knocks on their door they will be able to open it without hesitation and without apprehension or alarm.

These are the things the public has a right to expect from their police force, and these are the things that in Charleston we try very hard to provide. People sometimes say to me, You seem to have built a police force that really does deter and prevent crime more successfully than is the case in most communities. How do you do it? How do you recruit your people and what intangibles do you look for? How do you train the 367 men and women who presently make up the Charleston police force? How do you discipline them, motivate them, control them? What makes your police force different? Complete answers to such questions would probably fill a second book, but let me see what I can do in a single chapter.

To begin with, recruiting is no problem. We have the highest pay scale in the state, and this attracts people who also know that we operate efficiently and fairly. We do advertise in various periodicals, but at least two-thirds of our recruits come to us of their own volition. We try to take a broad approach. We're not just looking for blue-collar people. If a person has worked for the Charleston symphony in some capacity, or has a history of involvement in the NAACP, such things are a plus. The level of education is constantly rising; now we have 130 college graduates, over one-half of the force. (When I arrived in 1982, there were four or five officers who were functional illiterates. They were good men, actually, holdovers from World War II days when the armed services had siphoned off everyone else and the only way these fellows could be useful and get into uniform was to join the police.)

Today, some people come to us straight out of college, some from the military, some may already have had some police experience, some have not. (In a way I prefer recruits with no experience; it's easier to teach them our way of doing things.) Training these people is a two- or sometimes two-and-a-half-year process. Once they're on the payroll, they start out with four weeks of training inside the department. Candidates must pass a written examination, a physical agility test, two psychological tests, an oral interview, a polygraph test, and a complete medical examination to make sure they are free of such maladies as asthma, diabetes, AIDS, and so forth.

Next, they have eight weeks of training at the state police academy. Then for a year and a half they are on probation, working with more experienced officers. This is where the innate ability of the recruit—or lack of it—shows up. Those who have ability and dedication are rewarded. Those who don't are not. What we have in the Charleston Police Department is a meritocracy. Nothing else counts.

In a true meritocracy, seniority means nothing. Why should it? The fact that someone has been around longer than someone else doesn't mean he or she does the job better. Indeed, an active law-enforcer's effectiveness decreases with age. I'd be happy to see our recruits stay with us for five or six years and then move on, making room for younger, more active men and women. We stress physical fitness constantly. We have a fully equipped gymnasium for our people to use, and they use it. There's nothing more humiliating than to see an overweight, out-of-shape cop huffing and puffing as he tries to run down a criminal in a foot chase. Fortunately, many of the crooks are in poor shape too, from drug abuse or alcohol abuse. When a member of our speedy Flying Squad gets on the tail of these crooks, they have about as much chance as a rabbit trying to outrun a coyote.

I don't consider any newcomer trained until I'm satisfied that he or she is oriented to what is sometimes called "Uncle Reuben's mould" (that's me) or "the Charleston way." The Charleston way is a set of intangibles that range all the way from leadership on my part and the part of my ranking officers to the firm conviction among the rank and file that we are an elite law enforcement body, dedicated to the safety and welfare of the community, acutely conscious at every moment of the image of the Charleston Police Department and determined not only not to damage it but to do positive things at every opportunity to enhance it.

Where leadership is concerned, I think it's important not to emphasize but to blur the lines separating ranks and responsibilities. If you think of an organization in terms of management and labor, I think management should do some labor, and vice versa. For example, I go out and direct traffic sometimes. I also help move those sawhorse barriers that we use to set up police lines. I do these things because when the officers who usually do them see the chief doing them, they say to themselves, Hey, my job must be important—essential, really—because there's the chief doing it. Likewise some members of the "labor" force, who may well be as bright or brighter than some members of the "management" team, deserve the chance to use those brains.

A leader has to be forever looking for talent. For example, I know that an effective sergeant is constantly counseling less experienced officers; a lazy sergeant is not. Let's say I hear a sergeant saying to an officer, "Look, there's one thing you've got to remember in a foot chase. Stay right with the guy, as close behind him as you can get. If he ducks into a house, close in even faster, because he may have a weapon in that house. If he can get to that weapon, he can stab or shoot you before you know it. All he needs is four or five seconds. Now remember what I'm telling you!" When I hear a sergeant talk like that, I know he's a can-do, take-charge, dedicated guy, and I'll keep my eye on him for future promotion.

Not everyone in a blue uniform is dedicated. If people coming into the department ask me which are the "off days," meaning can they count on frequent weekends off, I answer them politely, but the question makes me wonder. I think the thing that burns me most in a police officer is inertia, the failure to take action in a crisis. I hate to hear cops sing the old bureaucratic song: There was nothing I could do. There's always something they can do; I want my officers to feel that the surest way to invite discipline is to do nothing. I say to them: "Don't give me that crap. If we want nothing done, we can get that for free. We don't have to pay you twenty-five grand a year to do it!"

Leaders have to support their followers. I stand behind my men and women in any controversy that arises
until it is proved beyond a doubt that the fault was
theirs. A police chief also has to be constantly aware of
the state of morale, the physical and emotional condition of the entire department. Most civilians do not
fully appreciate the strains and stresses involved in
police work. It is a difficult, dangerous, sometimes
exhausting, often nerve-wracking occupation, and we
try to make sure that our people are in condition to
meet such strains.

For instance, we have one particularly quiet precinct
with a low frequency of calls or crises. We call it, half
seriously, the "vacation precinct," and we often assign
officers who are showing signs of stress or battle fatigue
to this relatively uneventful sector of the city. It gives
them a chance to mellow out, ease up a bit, do some
thinking, stop going flat out, recharge their emotional
batteries. I assigned myself to that precinct last Christmas in order to let someone with children stay home
with his kids. I never had a single call, just rode around
in my patrol car, listening to the dispatcher—good dis-
patchers are a definite plus in any police department—
looking at the scenery and enjoying myself. The "vacation precinct" may sound like a goof-off assignment,
but it's not. It has tremendous therapeutic value, and
the proof is that, after a while, officers assigned become
charged up again and want to return to their normal,
more active duties.

In Charleston we have found it useful and effective
to divide our police force into two major divisions. The
First Force handles calls for service: a reported prowler,
a missing person, any complaint from a victim of a

crime. The Second Force—you might call it our shock troops—confronts the criminal element directly. The Second Force includes foot patrol, horse patrol, our Flying Squad, our Tactical Squad, our Vice Squad, and others. There are about 150 people in the First Force and some 100 in the Second Force.

The Second Force tends to be composed of officers with more experience than those in the First Force. Its mission is to confront criminals, chase them down, arrest them at every legitimate opportunity. Speed of response is of enormous importance. Not long ago in a major city in Texas a woman reporting a break-in called urgently for help. When the police arrived forty minutes later, she was dead. In Charleston, to minimize such tragedies, we have our access routes figured out in advance, designed to avoid possible delays from traffic jams, long trains at grade crossings, or other obstacles. In Charleston, in most cases, we can be on the scene of a crime in three minutes or less.

If a criminal runs away, we try to saturate the area with cops, not just rely entirely on one pursuing officer. The crook may run in any direction: east, west, north, south. If we have officers converging on him from all points of the compass, his chances of escaping are reduced to a minimum.

We want our pursuers to be relentless, too. Not long ago a five-time rapist tried to escape by ducking and hiding in a parking lot crammed with vehicles. To get him, our men ran across the hoods of a number of parked cars, scuffing them up quite a bit. It cost us about two thousand dollars to repaint those cars, but with a five-time rapist in our hands and out of action we figured it was worth it.

Recently, some police forces in other parts of the country have adopted a policy that they call "differential response." They classify incoming calls into categories: those that they feel require a response by a police officer in person and those that don't.

Their theory is that not every call from a citizen needs to be answered by a uniformed officer. If a bicycle disappears from a front porch, or if a car is stolen, a description of the missing property can be obtained over the telephone. No use going around to the house, is there? After all, the bicycle or car is gone. Better to use the officer's time on more serious matters. That's more efficient, right?

Wrong! Wrong because it weakens the invisible bond that should exist between the police and the public. Wrong because the person who has suffered the loss needs a display of concern and caring. The owner of a just-stolen car is usually somewhat traumatized and wants his questions answered by a visible human being, not an invisible and distant voice. He or she needs the reassurance of a blue uniform standing in the living room offering sympathy, if not an instant solution to the trouble.

That's why in Charleston we answer calls in person. Every single one. Under the "differential response" system, the victim of a crime feels like just an unfortunate statistic. The police are remote. They don't really care. And so if, later on, that same person happens to see a mugging or a purse snatching or some other crime being committed, chances are he or she won't bother to call it in. They don't care about me; why should I bother to help them?

A crime victim needs understanding and reassurance. A sympathetic cop can provide that. Once that bond is established between the police and the inhabitants of a town, police work instantly becomes easier because the citizen is now a strong ally in the war against the crooks.

Just the other day in a Charleston suburb a purse

snatcher grabbed a woman's pocketbook and ran. The call came quickly; the cops were on the scene in about three minutes. Of course, by that time the thief was out of sight, but an alert witness pointed out the way he had gone. As the patrol car moved in that direction, other people who had seen the fugitive running were out in the street signaling the direction he had taken. One citizen picked up the purse from the gutter where it had been flung. Two other young men actually pursued the robber, caught up with him, and by the time the patrol car arrived had him pinned against a railing. All the officer had to do was snap on the handcuffs. The point is, the officer didn't make the arrest; the community did. And the community did because its residents regarded the cops as friends and wanted to help them.

Our officers are trained to be around when things go badly, but we also want them to be around when things are going well. We don't want our people to be associated only with trouble; we want them sometimes to be symbols of good times. That's why our Police Athletic League organizes skateboard contests for kids. It also runs a soccer league. It sponsors a Boy Scout troop and even helps underprivileged youngsters keep up with their schoolwork. It aids crippled children. The money for these activities is raised by the officers themselves. The effort is good for the kids and good for the morale of the officers. They like being perceived in an affirmative role. A couple of years ago, when there was a terrible drought in the Midwest, our people loaded a police truck with hay and drove it, on their own time and at their own expense, to those suffering faraway farmers.

Discipline is strict in the CPD. We punish for every single infraction, every time. No second chances, no free shots. When punishment is certain, fewer punishments are needed. Punishment need not be loss of pay or privileges. It may mean simply holding an officer accountable for his wrongs. When something goes wrong there is a reason for it. It is not just "one of those things." Somebody dropped the ball. We let them know that we don't want the ball dropped again.

One problem common to most other police departments is abuse of sick leave. An officer calls in sick, but he or she is not really sick, just stealing some time off. We won't put up with that because it leaves a gap in the enforcement network that is difficult to fill on such short notice. So I say to my people, It doesn't matter what your salary is; if you're not here, what we're getting for your salary is zero. If you don't show up on your foot patrol beat, crimes are going to happen that wouldn't happen if you were there. If you're not in the saddle for horse patrol, some criminal is going to get away with something that you could have prevented. I realize that occasionally even police officers do get sick, but they get sick a lot less frequently if they know that abuse of sick leave will not be tolerated. Last year almost half of our entire force used no sick leave at all, and of those who took sick leave most claimed three days or less.

What about that ominous old phrase, bribery and corruption? It's not a problem with our people. Not that they're all plaster saints, but they are reasonably well paid, so the temptation to accept a bribe is lessened. Also, they know that if they are tempted and succumb, sooner or later—usually sooner—we are going to find out about it. Even if an anonymous and totally unsubstantiated phone call comes in accusing an officer of soliciting or taking a bribe, we let him know that such a call has been received. No other action; just the plain statement. Now he or she knows about it, and he knows that we know about it, and—true or false—it has a cautionary effect. Usually, it is false.

One of our traffic men had an approach to speeders that almost backfired on him. When he pulled them over and approached their car he would say sardonically, "Do you have sixty dollars?" What he meant was, Are you so rich that you can afford to pay sixty dollars to the city of Charleston as a fine for speeding? But it sounded to the driver like a come-on for a bribe. When this was reported to us we had a little talk with the officer, after which he was careful to refrain from asking hypothetical questions.

In Charleston our police force operates on three ten-hour shifts around the clock. The shifts overlap, of course, but this is deliberate. Some police departments try to get by with three eight-hour shifts, but because it takes time for the changeover, law enforcement sags at the point where the shifts meet. I know of one police force with a thousand officers. They divide their area into ten parts with a hundred assigned to each. They work eight-hour shifts, which leaves a window of vulnerability. The whole thing is too rigid. Criminals don't operate on such a neat and predictable schedule. Police forces can't afford to either; they have to stay flexible. For example, we know that most serious crimes are committed between 10 P.M. and 2 A.M., so we beef up our forces between those hours.

Members of our police force know that hours are long and requirements are demanding, but morale stays high. Unlike the situation that prevails in many other police departments, you don't have to come in at the bottom and laboriously work your way up the ladder. We have a lateral entry system in which a new employee can come in at any level, with rank and salary depending on education and previous experience. Salaries correspond strictly to rank. It's like the Army: a corporal gets a corporal's pay no matter what his assignment. If you're a lieutenant, you get what all the other lieutenants get. No one has a hammerlock on preferred working hours, either; weekends are rotated.

Our affirmative action program in the Charleston Police Department has never been challenged because it works to everyone's advantage. In making promotions we try to go primarily by merit, but if an officer is a woman or a member of a minority group, that factor is considered along with test scores and other yardsticks. If a member of a minority retires, we try to replace him or her with a member of the same minority. Fairness is the key. We don't want any member of the force to feel that he or she can never be promoted. Once a person loses all hope of promotion, performance goes down the drain.

In our ceaseless war against crime we try to use innovative and ingenious tactics. For example, if a foot patrolman sees a known burglar on his beat, he doesn't regard him with tolerance just because he's not burgling at the moment. He watches him like a hawk, ready to hand him a citation for any kind of minor infraction: jay-walking, littering, anything.

Well, you may say, that seems almost silly. Johnny the Burglar isn't going to show up in court in response to a summons for littering, is he? Of course not. Why, then, issue the summons? Because when he fails to show up, we can get the judge to issue a bench warrant for his arrest.

Armed with that bench warrant, we can make life miserable for our larcenous friend. We can stop Johnny wherever we see him; we can search his person, search his car; we can enter his house looking for stolen goods. We don't have to wait for probable cause. That summons for littering was not just to keep our streets clean.

It has now been converted into an engraved invitation to Johnny the Burglar to remove himself from our midst and carry on his trade—if he must—elsewhere. I suppose the people who live in Elsewhere, USA, hate me for this. My answer is that there's nothing to prevent them from making life miserable for crooks in their own community.

Indeed, I confess I've had it said to me, "Well, you don't really put most crooks behind bars. You just chase 'em out of Charleston." I'll plead guilty to that. With pleasure. I want those crooks someplace else. And that's where we drive 'em: someplace else. That's one reason why—despite substantial population growth—the number of burglaries in Charleston is the lowest in thirty years.

In Charleston, we clear with an arrest sixty percent of all cases of armed robbery. In other words, an armed robber has a six in ten chance of getting caught in Charleston. As for burglaries, we clear with an arrest three times more than the national average, or thirty-nine percent of the cases. That might not sound like much, unless you look at the national average, which is *thirteen percent.* In sex assaults, we have an eighty-eight percent success rate of clearing these cases with an arrest. And *all* homicide cases, virtually without exception, are cleared with an arrest.

I hope in this chapter I haven't been blowing the horn too loudly for the ranks of the Charleston Police Department. I'm just trying to give credit where it belongs, to 367 men and women in blue uniforms who do a superb job and do it bravely, tirelessly, and effectively. In the city of Charleston, South Carolina, our designated battleground, they are winning the war against crime.

Is that worth sounding a trumpet for? You know it is. Is that something that could start a crusade against crime all throughout the United States? You know that, given the will, the know-how, and the leadership, this nation is strong enough and angry enough to take back our streets and keep them vermin-free for the rest of our lives.

26
Taking Back Our Streets: What We Can Do

The more you observe and try to deal with the problem of crime in the United States, the more certain one thing becomes: there is no single solution. Nobody has one neat and final answer. There isn't any.

But this doesn't mean that the situation is hopeless. There are step-by-step solutions involving many people: police, city planners, judicial reformers, educators, sociologists, plus many ordinary citizens who are learning how to cooperate with their police and also how to protect themselves when the police are not on hand to protect them.

It's the *cumulative* effect of all these step-by-step solutions that offers the real hope of taking back our streets. Put enough of them together and you begin to reverse what otherwise looks like an irresistible tide of criminality.

Some of these solutions are low-key, long-term efforts. In many cities, for example, low-income housing projects have become a miserable mix of welfare families, drug pushers, unmarried mothers, fatherless kids, and general despair. The massive nature of the ghetto stifles any attempt at improvement. Why pick up trash when nobody else does? Why plant a flower when you know it will be trampled or stolen? Why even try?

Here in Charleston we are not building massive low-income housing projects any more. We're taking two units, four units, perhaps eight units and planting them in non-ghetto surroundings. The houses thus planted look just like the other houses in the neighborhood, but in these units the rent is still seventy dollars per month while the houses on either side may rent for four hundred or five hundred dollars. The rooms and the appliances in these subsidized houses may be a bit smaller, but the only way you can tell from the outside that a low-income family lives there is that there may be no car in the parking space, while next door there may be a Chevy or a Buick or even a BMW.

Despite glum predictions, there has been no resistance to such a plan from the more affluent neighbors, because what they fear is the massiveness of the ghetto with all its concentrated crime and squalor and poverty. They are not afraid of a few individuals who, having escaped from the ghetto themselves, want very much to imitate and maintain the standards of the neighborhood where they now find themselves. Children of these families, when asked where they live, are delighted not to have to say they live in a project. They can name a street in a respectable neighborhood. They play with children whose fathers—unheard of phenomenon—come home every night. They may still go to public schools, not private ones; their mothers may ride the bus, not drive to work. But they have escaped from a hopeless environment to a brighter one. Is the incidence of crime among these kids going to decrease? You know it is!

Improvements are coming too (slowly, I'll admit) in the way police forces are deployed and handled. Often in my travels I hear other police chiefs say, "We can't do the job right in our town because we don't have enough officers. And when we ask for more we're told there is no money."

I am not moved to tears by such sad tales. The number of men and women you have on a police force is far less important than the way those officers are used.

Obviously, if you're talking about a city, you can't have a cop on every corner. Which is okay because not every corner needs a cop. If you try anything like that, you just dilute the forces available to you until they're useless. It's like the old illustration: if you squeeze a lemon into a fifty-five gallon drum of water, what have you got? Nothing. But if you squeeze the same lemon into a pint of water you've got lemonade.

The way to make your police force count is to concentrate it in some crime-ridden area, occupy that area, saturate it with police, show the crooks you mean business, clear them out of that neighborhood, demonstrate who's boss. Once you've dominated an area, and the crooks know it, they will move on and you can continue to control that area with a greatly reduced presence. That, essentially, is what we've done in Charleston. We've taken one area after another away from the crooks, and we haven't given any back. Not one.

The best way for a police chief to get authorization for more officers is to demonstrate that you're doing a good job with the forces you have. I've never had such a request turned down here in Charleston, because the mayor knows that I don't make such a request unless there is a very good reason (for example, when I requested officers and launches to make up the Harbor Patrol) and that the additional resources will be used in an efficient and cost-effective way.

In Washington, D.C., and in other cities too, there are places where drug sellers will descend upon you in droves. "Hey, man, try some of this!" "My stuff is better, it's cheaper, it's purer!" That street intersection, that block belongs to the pushers. Why? Because nobody so far has made a determined effort to take it away from them.

If I were in charge of law enforcement in a city like that, I would bring in fifteen, twenty, thirty men. I'd have all the equipment I needed: paddy wagons, backup forces, instant police communications. I'd have officers assigned to drive paddy wagons full of these guys down to headquarters with jail cells waiting for them. I'd occupy that area so thoroughly that by sundown the pushers would be saying to one another, "This street corner, this intersection, this block doesn't belong to us anymore. It belongs to the cops. It's their turf now. And we're not going to try to take it back because we know we'll get our ears pinned back if we do."

This strategy of occupying enemy territory certainly isn't new; it goes back to the Romans. That's how the U.S. cavalry took the West away from the Indians. They'd establish a fort, send out patrols, set up outposts, gradually subdue one area after another. They knew it wasn't necessary to deploy numerous troops to hold a territory once their dominance was established. Just small outposts not too far from the main base of operations.

Look around: you'll see this concept in operation everywhere. Take a high-rise building in some affluent part of New York City. There's the doorman, sitting behind a switchboard that connects him to every apartment in the building. Maybe he has TV monitors as well, so he can see who walks down the corridors or gets on or off the elevators. What's he doing, really? He's *occupying* that key position in the building. He's making sure that hostile forces don't get through. It only takes one man, but his being there means security for several hundred tenants. Same thing is true of a security guard in a bank or a department store. The concept is so effective that today the number of security personnel in the country is greater than all the police forces combined.

Another step-by-step solution to the crime problem is to use auxiliary police: carefully selected and trained volunteers acting as backup to regular police officers. We have had such a volunteer force in Charleston for years; some of our best officers in the Charleston Police Department today started out as volunteers and found the work so fascinating that they gave up their regular jobs to come aboard permanently. At the moment we have twenty-eight of these trained volunteers who work twenty hours a week in patrol cars, sometimes with a regular officer, more often by themselves. They are in uniform with guns, caps, badges, and so on provided by us. If a citizen going out of town asks us to keep an eye on his or her house, these volunteers will do it. They cost the department nothing, and they perform a very useful function.

People ask me sometimes how I would control these really wild drug gangs that kill one another and innocent bystanders in cities like Los Angeles and Miami and New York. Certainly I can offer no foolproof solution to a problem that has become gigantic, but I do know this: you can't just sit back and wait for violence to happen and then try to deal with it. To be reactive isn't good enough; you have to be proactive. You have to take measures to defuse trouble before it starts. In the case of street gangs, this means going into their haunts, invading their meeting places, using informers whenever you can. It means following them, talking to them, patting them down, searching their cars, confiscating their weapons. The object is not to arrest them or drag them into court. That instantly raises questions of probable cause. The object is to keep them off balance, keep them under surveillance, keep them disorganized, because it's only when they are organized that they become dangerous.

These tactics work with big gangs or little ones. The other day here in Charleston, a call came in saying that four teenagers had been spotted carrying clubs and lengths of lead pipes, which a concerned citizen rightfully considered alarming. I heard the call on my patrol car radio and went to investigate myself. Two other patrol cars also converged on the group, who were not happy about thus being accosted. Where were they going? Nowhere. Where did they get the pieces of pipe? Over there behind a fence. (Investigation showed no such cache of pipes.)

"Well," I said to them, "isn't this wonderful? We need some pipes like that, and we've been looking everywhere, and now you've saved us the trouble of looking any further. You really should get a reward!" So we took the pipes. "Where do you guys live? We'll give you a ride home."

They didn't want a ride home, but we put one of them in each of the patrol cars and drove them home where their arrival in such high style was sure to be noticed by neighbors or parents. The fourth one we left to walk home. In a minigang of four, he was a potential menace. Alone he was quite harmless. No big deal? Of course not. But it's this kind of proactive rather than reactive approach that has kept gang activity in Charleston to a minimum.

People often ask me, somewhat apprehensively, about what they perceive as the rise of vigilantism in America. Like most words, vigilantism can mean different things to different people. Actually it comes from a Spanish word meaning *guard* or *watchman*.

My dictionary defines a vigilante as "a member of a volunteer committee of citizens organized to suppress and punish crime summarily (as when the processes of law appear inadequate)." The phrase in parentheses is important, because when citizens band together or take action singly to "suppress or punish" crime without waiting for police action, almost always it's because they perceive a threat to their persons or their property that isn't being addressed.

Sometimes this citizen action is relatively passive, such as when citizens in Florida (and elsewhere) barricade streets without authorization to make access to their residential area more difficult for intruders. Sometimes the action is quite violent, as in the case of the two men in Detroit mentioned earlier, who burned down a house in their neighborhood because they claimed it was a distribution center for crack. Technically they were guilty of arson, but when tried, they were acquitted. Their lawyers showed that drug-related gunfights in the street had endangered the lives of neighborhood children, and that numerous complaints to police had produced no remedial action.

In New York City a group of self-appointed monitors of street crime known as Guardian Angels has been the subject of much controversy. Many subway riders have said they are glad to see these young men and women in their red berets riding in the same car with them because they feel safe from muggers or the type of aggressive behavior from other passengers that led to the widely publicized Bernhard Goetz incident. (I think myself that Goetz was just defending himself when he opened fire; he believed himself to be in danger, and very likely he was.)

My feeling about the Guardian Angels is that they came into being in response to a need that wasn't being met. Coming from the streets themselves, they are more likely to understand the tactics and mentality of street thugs than officers in a patrol car—a steel-and-glass cage that definitely limits their view of what is going on around them. You can't get a patrol car into a subway.

When people ask me what I would do if the Guardian Angels came to Charleston, I reply that I would try to recruit the best of them for the CPD. I would check carefully to make sure that none had a police record or presented a health hazard. Then I would recruit them and bring them under the control and jurisdiction of the city of Charleston. If they refused recruitment, I would not tolerate them in my area of responsibility because I know our own people are capable of handling the street crime problem here without any unsolicited help.

Sometimes I think fear of being labeled a vigilante makes ordinary citizens hesitant to defend themselves. Many people are unsure of their rights when it comes to protecting their homes or places of business against an intruder. The fact is, a law-abiding person may use force, even deadly force, against someone intent on robbing or harming him or her.

Not long ago here in Charleston three men decided to rob a jewelry store. They broke into the store at about eight in the morning, quite sure they would find it empty because a sign on the door said clearly, "Open at 10 A.M." Not being businesspeople themselves, it never occurred to the crooks that the owner or his helpers might come to work earlier to prepare for the day's business. They posted two lookouts to watch for cops while the third broke a window and went inside to steal what he could.

Actually the broken window triggered an alarm, and the cops were on their way to the scene. But before they could arrive, the owner himself drove up with his wife in the car. The lookouts paid no attention because obviously he was not a cop and they figured the store wouldn't open until ten. They thought their robbery was proceeding very nicely.

But the owner had a gun in his car. He had a right to have it because he often carried cash or valuable jewelry. Seeing the broken window, he jumped out of the car with his gun, entered the store, caught the intruder, and in his righteous wrath whacked his captive repeatedly over the head with the barrel of his gun. He really did a number on that robber. When the cops arrived, almost in a matter of seconds, nobody was gladder to see them than the crook, who by then had a broken nose, a lacerated scalp, possibly a fractured jaw, and other poignant reminders that breaking into a man's store and stealing his merchandise does, after all, have its risks.

The lookouts ran away, of course, when they saw the police. But we caught them later; once you have one of such a trio, eventually you'll nab them all. I thought perhaps the owner of the store might have displayed a little less zeal, but I also figured—knowing what I did about the courts—that this was the only real punishment the crook was ever likely to receive. So I had no intention of arresting the jeweler. If he had spied the criminal in another place a week later and had assaulted him then, that would have been a different matter. And certainly I would not tolerate such action on the part of any of my officers. But a man defending his own livelihood on his own property and reacting with justifiable anger against the intruder was not going to be arrested by me. If the prosecutor wanted to make an issue of it—thereby incurring the wrath of a sympathetic public—then he could do so. But I knew the reaction of a jury would be much like my own.

There are other step-by-step solutions to the crime problem that will never be attempted because they would run squarely into massive financial interests. Take car thefts, for example. Before a car leaves the factory it would be very easy to etch the Vehicle Identification Number (VIN) in small numerals on the windshield, on the windows, on the fenders, on the bumpers, everywhere, so that if the car were stolen, or even stolen and dismantled, it would be much easier to trace. But this is not likely to happen because the automobile industry knows that someone who has a car stolen is almost always a red-hot customer for a new car. Or at least a secondhand car. Who wants to tamper with a ready-made market like that?

Some individuals, too, make a good living and a lawful living out of crime. I know a lawyer (another one of those!) who specializes in defending drunk drivers. One bit of advice he does pass along is to carry an onion with them at all times while they're driving. If they take a quick bite when a cop pulls them over, they might be able to distort the results of a Breathalyzer test. Nice fellow.

He came to see me the other day because he was about to defend a Navy captain we had charged with drunk driving. There was no doubt about the evidence in the case; we even had videotapes of his wildly erratic driving. The lawyer said he had come to Caesar (meaning me) because he had no other place to turn. If I would drop the charges, he said, I would save this fine fellow's career. If he were convicted, his admiral had indicated that he would not be entrusted with the command of a naval vessel which, the lawyer hinted, might even be a nuclear submarine. Besides, he had such a nice family, nice wife, nice children, and so on.

I was not moved by any of this. I pointed out that a drunken four-striper behind the wheel of a car could kill a pedestrian just as dead as the rawest recruit. Besides, if the captain had had no consideration for his own family's welfare, why should I? So I turned him down. I don't believe in second chances. I wish our society would embrace the same attitude, but we live in a culture that not only tolerates second chances, but seems resigned to them no matter how dire the consequences may be. The captain of the Exxon tanker that ran aground in Alaska was a man with a known drinking problem. How many second chances was he given before the disaster occurred that just about ruined the coastline of Alaska?

Where teenage drunk driving is concerned, we learned very quickly when we lowered the drinking age to eighteen that the consequences in terms of traffic accidents and fatalities were disastrous. It sounded nice to say that if a kid is old enough to serve in the armed forces and perhaps die for his country, he should be old enough to take a drink. But young drivers tend to be reckless. They often feel invulnerable behind a wheel, and with alcohol clouding their judgment they became such a menace that the laws had to be changed and the drinking age rolled back to twenty-one. A badly needed measure you might say. Even then I had tavern owners plead with me to use whatever influence I might have to leave the drinking age at eighteen. The ones nearest the naval base and the campus of the Citadel, the military college in Charleston, moaned the loudest, claiming it would ruin their business. I hope it did.

The most effective sanction against teenage drivers who are picked up driving under the influence of alcohol is to suspend or withdraw their driving licenses. Driving an automobile is a privilege, not a right. (In Sweden, I'm told, the *first* time an offender is convicted he or she loses his license *permanently!*) Suspending teenagers' licenses is an effective form of punishment because they are in the age group most likely to be caught if they try to drive without one.

A powerful weapon against drunk drivers is shame or embarrassment. I read the other day of a judge in Florida who ordered first time DWI offenders to pay for their mistake by placing a signed advertisement, complete with photograph, in the local newspaper. The ad included the statement: "I apologize to all the people of this community for driving impaired." A probation officer said they found that people would prefer to pay a large fine or even go to jail rather than face such humiliation. "It's a nightmare," muttered one person so sentenced. Exactly. That was the whole idea. Another partial solution, perhaps, but with enough partial solutions progress can be made.

Any police officer—any serious-minded citizen—will tell you that we need to step up penalties and sanctions against law-breakers everywhere. Street criminals now regard the judicial system with contempt. Members of Congress ignore it. Take the thirty-five million people who are said to be social users of drugs in this country. Obviously you can't put them all in jail. You can try to educate them about the dangers of using drugs, but they probably won't listen. You can point out that it's their money that fuels the horrible drug trade and causes endless misery and death. But they're not likely to be all that sensitive where matters of conscience are concerned. You need to add the element of *fear*, fear of what will happen to them if they're caught buying or using or possessing illegal drugs.

Recently in a South Carolina school system, it was noticed that one female teacher seemed incapable of sitting through a faculty meeting. No doubt faculty meetings are boring, but this woman's response seemed to indicate that something else was wrong. It was; she was hooked on cocaine. She couldn't get through a two-hour faculty meeting without a fix.

In a case like that, why wouldn't it make sense to revoke her teacher's certificate immediately for—say—six months? If a lawyer is caught, why not suspend his license to practice for a year? Or a doctor, or a CPA, or any licensed practitioner? There should be no probation for a first offense. There should be none of this nonsense about hating the sin and loving the sinner. There should be no second chances. The law should have teeth, and it should bite.

In police work you learn the hard way that giving second chances can backfire. Years ago, I remember, I was called to a house where a domestic dispute was going on. Husband and wife were indeed having a noisy quarrel, which is why the neighbors called the police. While calming them down, I noticed a pistol lying on a table. It was the man's pistol; he had a right to have it in his home. Since he had not pointed the gun at anyone, including his wife, I decided to leave it where it was. I gave them a stern warning to behave themselves, and left.

Forty minutes later I was called back to the same house, where the quarrel had erupted again. But this time the pistol was not lying on a table. When I opened the door, it was pointed straight at my head, about two feet from my face, held by the householder whose fury was unmistakable. Scared? I was petrified! I remember looking at that round black opening in the muzzle of the gun and waiting for the tongue of flame that would have ended all my worldly problems for good. I was very lucky. The shot never came. But ever since then I have been very touchy about giving second chances, especially where guns are concerned.

Not long ago a mistake like that cost a police chief in another South Carolina town his life. I know that civilians sometimes wonder why police routinely put handcuffs on persons arrested for relatively minor offenses like shoplifting. Such suspects have been known to complain loudly too. But the reason is a compelling one: it's to prevent the suspect from suddenly producing a concealed weapon and using it on the arresting officer. If the handcuffs are embarrassing, or even pinch a little bit, that's too bad. There's a wry saying among policemen, Better tried by twelve than carried by six. It's better to risk being charged with overzealousness than find yourself dead.

Which is what happened to the police chief in this case. He had arrested a couple on drug charges; the girl was just a teenager. He didn't handcuff her, perhaps because he had been criticized in the past for being a little too quick to handcuff women. This time his failure to take precautions cost him his life. The girl shot him with a pistol the couple had. To make sure he was dead, they shot him again with his own service revolver. Then they vanished.

There was a somewhat bizarre sequel to this episode. A family in Charleston took pity on a young couple who said their truck had broken down. They had no money, no place to stay. They had a shotgun that they offered to sell. Their benefactors didn't want the gun, but they did say the young couple could spend the night. They felt no apprehension until by chance, turning on the evening news, one member of the family heard about the murder of the police chief. A description of the suspects was also broadcast, and it matched almost perfectly the appearance of the two overnight guests. A surreptitious and frantic call brought the police quickly. They surrounded the house and managed to spirit some members of the family out of a bedroom window. But the young couple was still inside, presumably cop-killers, armed and extremely dangerous.

I was at home, trying to shrug off jet lag from a return trip from Australia, when the call came in. I left immediately for the scene, giving orders to do nothing until I got there. I wanted to be the first police officer through the door of that house. I can imagine only one thing worse than being shot and killed by a cornered criminal, and that would be ordering one of my own men through a door and seeing him shot while I stood outside. So I went first, with drawn gun, and we pounced on these suspects, who looked terrified and offered no resistance. They offered no resistance for a very good reason: they were not the cop-killers at all. They were just a young couple with a broken-down truck who happened to look a lot like the real killers.

When everyone calmed down, it was obvious that the Good Samaritans no longer wanted to have these particular visitors, innocent or not. I felt we had frightened the youngsters badly, so I suggested that we put them up for a couple of nights at a motel, courtesy of the Charleston Police Department. We drove them back to the town of Summerville, a few miles away, where their truck was being repaired, shook their hands, and wished them well. I guess they were glad to see us go. A few days later the real culprits in the murder of the police chief turned themselves in.

The list of step-by-step solutions to the crime problem is already long, and as public indignation rises it will grow longer still. Sensible men and women everywhere know that the police need help in this ceaseless war. Guardians in blue cannot be everywhere at all times. Sometimes citizens have to take action themselves, like the teachers at Public School 70 in the Bronx who, tired of having their automobiles constantly vandalized, contributed twenty dollars apiece each month to hire a plainclothes guard to watch their cars. They were not happy about paying to protect themselves, but incidents of vandalism dropped almost to zero.

Whether such remedial action seems necessary or not, it is still possible for any citizen, male or female, to become a partial solution in the attitudes he or she adopts:

By facing the crime problem with realism and tough-minded anger.

By refusing to accept environmental conditioning as an excuse for wrongdoing.

By objecting to wrist-tap sentencing and automatic probation for first offenders.

By clamoring for stronger and swifter penalties for lawbreakers.

By teaching accountability to children and demanding it from all others.

By realizing that a society that flinches from punishing evil in its midst runs the risk of self-extinction.

By doing everything possible to change the climate of permissiveness and inertia that clogs our courts and paralyzes our whole judicial system.

By refusing to be part of the hopelessness that says that nothing can be done.

We have almost a quarter of a billion people in this land of ours. If even ten percent work at seeking step-by-step solutions, the crime problem will begin to shrink to manageable proportions.

It can be done.

I know, because I have seen it happen here.

27
Now They Call It Saintsville

The other day a friend of mine from Savannah paid me a visit. He came by train and asked a black cab driver at the station to bring him to police headquarters. On the way he got to talking with the driver. "How are things in Charleston these days?" he asked. "How's the crime situation?"

"Crime situation?" answered the driver. "What crime? Now they're calling it Saintsville!"

My friend and I got a smile out of that. Charleston isn't the exclusive habitat of saints, by any means. But the remark reflected the change that has taken place in the last few years and how our own citizens regard that change. Crime is no longer a dominant factor here; it's not the major menace that it once was.

All sorts of statistics bear me out. Armed robberies are down more than sixty percent—from 365 in 1982, the year I came, to 165 last year. Burglaries are down by half; homicides by half. Auto thefts, aggravated assaults all down, although the population of the city has increased. Most of these improvements have been brought about without the expenditure of significant additional funds.

So we have had our local successes, but I am well aware that the problem of crime in the United States remains a gigantic one that poses far more questions than answers.

How can our schools and churches best approach the enormous task of planting a renewed sense of values and accountability in our young people? What is going to restore the integrity of the family and halt the torrent of illegitimate births? How can indifferent citizens be persuaded to join the police in the war against crime? What can be done about the (to me) hopelessly naive efforts of the rehabilitation industry to make choir boys out of hardened criminals who long ago chose and will continue to choose crime as a calculated method of obtaining desired goals? Is there any hope for our judicial system, a jumble of antiquated procedures so hopelessly out of touch with the realities of crime today that at times it seems almost totally obsolete?

I'm a police chief, not a social reformer, and I don't pretend to have answers to such enormous questions. But in these challenging years in Charleston, I have learned that when a police department does its job the way it should be done, social reform follows right along. If other cities would try to do what Charleston has done in this one area, they would find that many of their other problems would become more manageable.

Recently Mayor Joseph P. Riley said that in Charleston major crimes are at their lowest point in twenty years. This is truly remarkable when you consider what has happened elsewhere. And the mayor should take a lot of the credit too. Much of our success is based on the support and encouragement he has given me.

Probably the remark I treasure most came from an occasional visitor to our city. "You know," he said, "I see all sorts of improvement in Charleston these days: race relations, cultural activities, business growth. But what impresses me most is the faces of the people. They have a totally different look. They're more relaxed, happier, more confident. Those people are not afraid to walk the streets any more. The fear has gone."

Yes, the fear has gone.

Because we've taken back our streets.